ROOMS OF THEIR OWN

ROOMS OF THEIR OWN

Nino Strachey

National Trust

First published in the United Kingdom in 2018 by
Pitkin Publishing
43 Great Ormond Street
London
WC1N 3HZ

An imprint of Pavilion Books Ltd.

ISBN 978-1-84165-788-2

A CIP catalogue record for this book is available from the British Library.

10 9 8 7 6 5 4 3 2 1

Reproduction by Rival Colour Ltd
Printed and bound in Slovenia
Designed by Lee-May Lim and Tokiko Morishima

This book can be ordered direct from the publisher at www.pavilionbooks.com
Also available at National Trust shops, including www.nationaltrustbooks.co.uk

FRONT COVER: The fire screen by Duncan Grant and EMG Gramophone decorated by John Banting from Eddy Sackville-West's Music Room at Knole.
BACK COVER: From left to right; Eddy Sackville-West by Ian Campbell-Gray, 1920; Virginia Woolf by Vanessa Bell, 1934; Clare Atwood's portrait of Vita Sackville-West as Portia in Willam Shakespeare's *The Merchant of Venice*, c1932.
HALF TITLE PAGE: Tiles by Duncan Grant, commissioned by Virginia Woolf for Monk's House.
TITLE PAGE: The windowsill of Harold Nicolson's Sitting Room, Sissinghurst.
RIGHT: The Pale Green Turret Room at Knole, with the pink walls of the Music Room in the foreground.
PAGE 6: Clockwise from left; Eddy Sackville-West (seated left) at Sissinghurst with Harold Nicolson, Vita Sackville-West, Ben Nicolson (standing) and Nigel Nicolson; Virginia Woolf at Knole with Ben and Nigel Nicolson; Vita and Eddy with Clive Bell and Dorothy Wellesley (?) at Long Barn; Eddy with Virginia, Lytton Strachey (extreme right) and David Cecil at Garsington.

Contents

Introduction

In the deep blue turret room at Knole stands a battered tin trunk inscribed 'Edward Sackville-West: Various Papers'. Hoarded inside were the intimate records of lives lived at the heart of 1920s Bloomsbury. Lytton Strachey, James Strachey, Alix Strachey, Duncan Grant, David "Bunny" Garnett and Stephen Tomlin all stayed with Eddy at Knole. Two of these friends – Duncan Grant and Stephen Tomlin – became lovers, filling his rooms with the vibrant outpourings of Bloomsbury creativity. Eddy's first cousin Vita Sackville-West and her lover Virginia Woolf were equally at home in this world, their names permanently associated through the publication of *Orlando*. Set at Knole, Woolf's tribute to Vita created a hero/heroine who evades categorisations of sex and time, changing as the centuries progress.

Linked by an intimate web of relationships, Eddy, Virginia and Vita created homes in Kent and East Sussex which challenged contemporary conventions. Living in an England where homosexuality was illegal until 1967, Eddy's design choices were boldly counter-cultural. Lytton Strachey left a wry account of his 'ladylike apartments', where the walls were painted in Marie Laurencin pink, and decked with Duncan Grant male nudes. Vita Sackville-West found him 'mincing in black velvet' amidst an array of rapiers, crucifixes and coloured lights: mauve for the bedroom; green, red and yellow for each turret. As she reported to Harold Nicolson: 'I don't object to homosexuality, but I do hate decadence'. Virginia Woolf may have disapproved of Eddy's tendency to 'paint and powder', but she was equally committed to the Bloomsbury philosophy of sexual equality and freedom. She believed that every person had the right to live and love in the way that they chose, and her own rooms at Monk's House are filled with works of art produced by the queer cross-gender collaboration of Duncan Grant and Vanessa Bell. Their distinctive combination of bright colours, bold patterns and eclectic objects creates an atmosphere of comfort and informality. There is a sense that anything could happen in these Bloomsbury-inspired rooms. Eroticism and humour are never far from the surface.

Vita's interiors at Sissinghurst were more subtly subversive, looking back towards the grandeur of the Elizabethan age. Fulfilling Virginia's dictum that 'a woman must have money and a room of her own if she is to write fiction', Vita filled her Writing Room with the romantic relics of past lovers. Every object carries an associative memory: crystal rabbits from Violet Trefusis, paintings by Mary Campbell, furniture sourced by Virginia Woolf, illuminated manuscripts produced by Chris St John, embroideries worked by Gwen St Aubyn. Vita's happy marriage to Harold Nicolson sustained not only a love affair with his sister but a lifetime of same-sex relationships on both sides. As she wrote in 1920:

I hold the conviction that as the centuries go on, and the sexes become more nearly merged on account of their increasing resemblances ... such connections will to a very large extent cease to be regarded as merely unnatural, and will be understood far better.

Eddy Sackville-West's
Music Room at Knole.

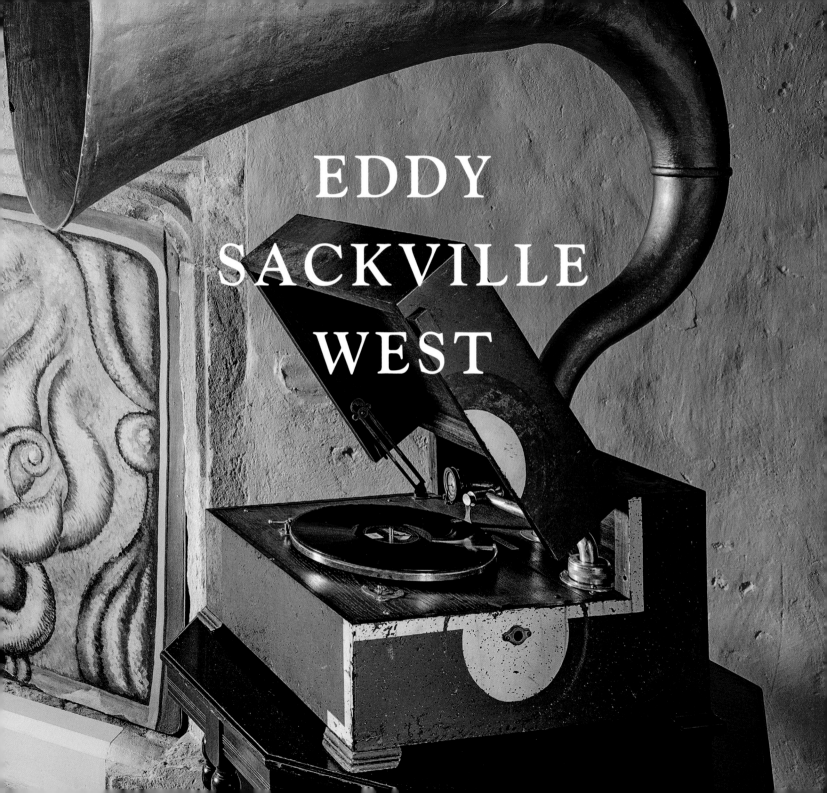

EDDY SACKVILLE WEST

Eddy Sackville-West, Knole, 1926

In January 1926 a young man was given an extraordinary opportunity: to furnish and decorate his own apartments in the Gatehouse Tower at Knole. Gaunt and rectangular, with four battlemented turrets, the 15th-century tower guards the entrance to the vast courtyard house beyond. As a small child, Eddy Sackville-West had toddled with his great-uncle 'in and out of the dim old rooms and passages, up and down stairs (one step at a time) and along what seemed miles of gallery', peeping into 'the shadowy interior of a huge Caroline four-poster bed hung with crimson silk' or 'a tall Meissen vase painted with a design of red chrysanthemums'. Although Eddy was happy to take his pick from the Sackville heirlooms, the suite of rooms he created at Knole are strikingly personal and contemporary in feel, making a clear statement about his taste and sexuality.

At 25, Eddy was already well known in Bloomsbury circles. He had published a critically acclaimed novel, *Piano Quintet*, and performed at Bloomsbury parties. Admired for his beauty, his wit, and his musical talent, Eddy carefully curated his own image. Photographs show his large violet eyes downcast, with hair swept distinctively across an arched forehead, and artfully applied make-up. His clothes and jewellery were exquisite and his sensibilities acute. Wracked with pain from hereditary telangiectasia, he suffered from hyperaesthesia, an abnormal sensitivity to all physical sensations, which left him feeling suspended between life and death. Virginia Woolf may have written *Orlando* in honour of his first cousin Vita, but elements of her hero are purely Eddy: 'He had eyes like drenched violets, so large that the water seemed to have brimmed in them and widened them; and a brow like the swelling of a marble dome pressed between the two blank medallions which were his temples ... Sights disturbed him ... sights exalted him – the birds and the trees; and made him in love with death.'

Eddy's design choices at Knole were guided by two very different aesthetics. On one side stood the bold contrasting colours of Bloomsbury, championed by his two key lovers of 1926: the sculptor Stephen Tomlin and the painter Duncan Grant. On the other, the macabre delights of 1890s decadence. As an 18-year-old schoolboy, Eddy had discovered Huysmans' *À Rebours*, the bible of French decadent literature. He had sworn that one day he would retreat alone to a house in the countryside, living in an artistic world of his own creation, wearing black velvet. Eddy's rooms at Knole were completed in May 1926, and Vita Sackville-West's horrified description to Harold Nicolson gives a flavour of the extreme reactions they could inspire: 'Darling, his rooms are rather awful. He has a pale mauve light in his bedroom. Then the three stone turret rooms ... are *eingerichtet* with a sort of ninety-ish affectation – a green light in one, a red light in another, a yellow light in the third; a rapier propped up in the corner, a crucifix on the wall ... And Eddy himself mincing in black velvet ... I don't object to homosexuality, but I do hate decadence. And it is a nasty fungoid growth on Knole of all places.'

RIGHT: Eddy Sackville-West in characteristic pose: violet eyes downcast, hair swept back from the 'marble dome' of his forehead.

ABOVE: Eddy Sackville-West sitting in a marble basin at Knole. Photographed by John Banting, 1927.

ABOVE AND LEFT:
Eddy Sackville-West posing with garden urns at Knole. Photographed by John Banting 1927.

ABOVE: Eddy in the garden at Long Barn. Photographed by Vita Sackville-West, 1927.

*For Eddy with my love — Eva Herrmann
Sauvey ½te Trinité. November 1933 —*

ABOVE: Eddy Sackville-West reclining on a daybed, wearing his distinctive jewellery:
gold bracelets, and Lady Betty Germain's ring from Knole. By Eva Herrman, 1933.

The Cult of the Effeminate
Oxford, 1920–1922

Eddy's schoolboy fascination with decadence developed under the influence of his Oxford contemporaries. At the start of his second year, Eddy formed a trio with John Strachey, whose father owned *The Spectator*, and John Rothenstein, son of the artist William Rothenstein. In his memoir *Summer's Lease*, Rothenstein paints a vivid picture of the prevailing aesthetic: 'this cult of the effeminate did not necessarily denote effeminacy in the generally accepted sense, nor even homosexuality, ubiquitous though this was … it was the product of several causes, not the least of which was the defiant assertion of the dandified intellectual (or "aesthete" as he was called) in the face of the formerly hectoring athlete, or "hearty"'.

Rothenstein's world was transformed through a bold aesthetic act. By painting his rooms gleaming white, and filling his walls with the works of Max Beerbohm and Augustus John, Rothenstein made himself as 'conspicuous as a white whale', causing 'a mild ripple of interest throughout the College; it even began to be whispered that I must be a homosexual. Although I went to much trouble to make my surroundings reflect my taste, without other motive than delight in the possession of rooms of my own and of exceptional beauty, they became a setting, almost as soon as they were ready, for an entirely altered way of life.'

This new way of life involved long evenings of 'bridge, baccarat, scandalous talk and music', and new friends like the beautiful Prendie (Jeffrey Prendergast) who pulled a white woollen lamb down the street, and was once found weeping for his lost allure.

Eddy, Strachey and Rothenstein featured prominently in this circle. In spring 1922 the trio spent three weeks in Vienna. Rothenstein recalled how Eddy's hypersensibilities, always the source of respectful amusement to his friends, were raised to their highest pitch by music. 'One night, at the conclusion of a Wagner opera which to me had seemed interminable, I made a movement of relief which caused my chair to creak. Eddie [sic] winced as though pierced by a hatpin. "Really Johnny, it's too bad," he said in his flat, cold voice, "that awful noise has spoilt the whole effect, now I've got to listen to it all again tomorrow night."'

John Strachey was equally distinctive. His sister Amabel arrived at Magdalen College to find him breakfasting on chocolate cake and crème de menthe, resplendent in brocade dressing gown and red Morocco slippers. He combined complete contempt for public opinion with a love of cricket. Eddy treasured a photograph of John in cricket whites, possibly taken on the day when he went into bat for Magdalen wearing a large French peasant hat, profusely ornamented with trailing pink ribbons. 'Just look what that bastard Strachey's got on his head,' snarled one unsympathetic spectator. Soon afterwards Strachey was writing to Rothenstein – 'we have got to give up this 90-ish way in which we have been living'.

LEFT: Portrait of Eddy Sackville-West, painted by his Oxford friend Ian Campbell-Gray, 1920.

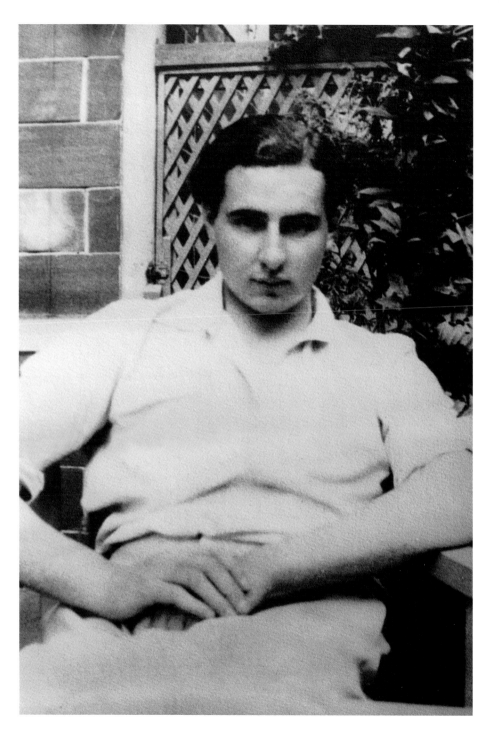

ABOVE: *During a performance of 'The Rheingold' Mr Sackville-West's neighbour whistles the tune –* cartoon of Eddy by John Rothenstein, 1922.

RIGHT: Eddy's photograph of John Strachey in cricket whites, Oxford, 1922.

LEFT: John Rothenstein in his rooms at Worcester College, Oxford, 1921.

Decadence Meets Bloomsbury

Oxford, 1922–1923

Eddy remained loyal to his decadent roots right through the 1920s, proclaiming his fascination with death and all its associated macabre trappings. But from 1922 a new influence came to the fore. Many different explanations have been offered for Eddy's introduction to Bloomsbury, but the most likely source was his relationship with John Strachey. John first appears in Eddy's diaries in July 1920, when the pair spent time on holiday in Paris. Eddy found the Folies Bergère 'disgustingly improper and indecent', and was sickened when a 'femme de mauvaise vie' took his arm in the foyer; 'As John says, I don't really come for the *actualité*'. Eddy was less squeamish about the gay bars they visited together in Vienna in March 1922; keen to share their experiences, they poured out their excitement to John's cousin Lytton Strachey, who replied dismissively, 'Oh, do you like that sort of thing?'

Through John, Eddy connected into a family at the heart of Bloomsbury. Under the editorship of John's father, *The Spectator* had become a source of employment for countless Stracheys. Lytton and his brother James (the first English translator of Freud) had both been regular contributors, while their cousin Duncan Grant produced exhibition reviews. And *The Spectator* was to prove a safe haven for John and Eddy when they both dropped out of Oxford without taking their degrees, moving into a London flat on the Cromwell Road with the aim of becoming great writers.

Thanks to their Bloomsbury connections, John and Eddy had already caught the eye of literary hostess Lady Ottoline Morrell. They soon

ABOVE: 'Undergraduates', Garsington Manor, June 1922: John Rothenstein, second from left; John Strachey, centre, with hands on hips; Eddy Sackville-West, second from right.

joined the host of promising Oxford undergraduates bidden to one of her summer garden parties at Garsington Manor. Lytton Strachey and Duncan Grant were both present during John and Eddy's first visit to Garsington in June 1922. Lady Ottoline recorded the young men in a series of captivating photographs, and John Rothenstein left a spellbound account of the day:

ABOVE: Eddy's first visit to Garsington Manor, June 1922. Seated, left to right: Eddy, John Rothenstein, Helen Anrep, John Strachey, William Stead. Standing: Julian Morrell (Ottoline's daughter) and L.P. Hartley.

One hot Sunday afternoon in the summer of 1922 John Strachey, Edward Sackville-West, David Cecil and I had been invited to their house. On arrival we hesitated at an open french [sic] window that gave upon a lawn, at the far side of which a tea-party was in progress. We hesitated because the lawn was not so wide that we could not discern among the tea drinkers the figures of Lytton Strachey, Aldous Huxley and Duncan Grant, as well as that, so awe-inspiring at a first encounter, of our hostess, and

this modest patch of grass seemed to us an alarmingly wide space to cross exposed to the gaze of so many august eyes. So it is that I still retain so clearly a picture of the group: Lytton Strachey limply inert in a low chair, head drooped forward and red beard pressed against chest, finger-tips touching the grass; Aldous Huxley talking, with his face raised upwards staring at the sun; Duncan Grant, pale-faced, with fine, untidy black hair, light eyes ready to be coaxed out of their melancholy, and Lady Ottoline,

ABOVE: Garsington Manor, June 1923. Clockwise from left: Eddy Sackville-West, Lytton Strachey (obscured), Virginia Woolf, Lord David Cecil.

wearing a dress of lilac silk more appropriate to some splendid Victorian occasion, and an immense straw hat. Our hesitation lasted only an instant, and presently we were seated in the circle around the tea-table.

Eddy's playfulness in front of the camera, and his first view of Duncan Grant, are captured beautifully in Ottoline's albums. A year later, Lady Ottoline provided a similar record of Eddy's first meeting with Virginia Woolf, who described Eddy as 'a tiny lap dog called Sackville-West ... he has a voice like a girl's and a face like a Persian cat's, all white and serious, with large violet eyes and fluffy cheeks'.

ABOVE: Garsington Manor, June 1923. From left to right: Lord David Cecil, Eddy Sackville-West, Virginia Woolf, Lytton Strachey.

RIGHT: 'Eddy courting death', taken by Lady Ottoline Morrell, Garsington Manor, 1924.

Bloomsbury Parties

London, 1924–1925

In January 1924 Eddy and John Strachey moved into Flat D, 45 Cromwell Road. This white stucco building opposite the Natural History Museum was Eddy's first independent home. Here he experimented with all the elements that were to become such distinctive features at Knole: music, contemporary art, and the constant presence of beautiful young men, painted, sculpted, or in the flesh. One of these young men, art critic Adrian Stokes, left a breathless account of his joy at sleeping in Eddy's room while he was away in Germany for psychoanalysis: 'I write this sitting at your desk, listening to a Mozart Quartette [sic] on your gramophone – and about to sleep in your bed ... I don't touch anything, and nothing of mine comes out of my box ... I do love all your things and they are so good for me. I know you much better while I live amongst your things and I treat them with great reverence.'

In London, Eddy was briefly exposed to radical activism. John Strachey was moving rapidly to the Left, contesting a Birmingham seat for the Labour party in 1924, and publishing his first book, *Revolution by Reason*, in 1925. Soon he was juggling two very different worlds: by day, he edited the *The Socialist Review*; by night he danced at drunken Bloomsbury parties with his lovely cousin Julia Strachey, future wife of Stephen Tomlin. Eddy was an equally decorative figure, picked out for special mention by Virginia Woolf: 'Karin's party came off last night ... 40 young Oxford men, and three very pretty girls ... Lytton gravitated to the 40 young men, and was heard booming and humming from flower to flower.' While Vanessa

ABOVE: Adrian Stokes, Eddy's lover, in 1924. In the words of a later admirer: 'he looked like a blond eagle and I fell for him. He was a painter, art-critic, and ballet lover.'

Bell chatted on a sofa with Stephen Tomlin, Leonard was 'set upon by little Eddie Sackville West [sic] who is as appealing as a kitten ... this poor boy, after pouring forth all his woes (all men confide in Leonard, especially such as love their own sex) sat by mistake down

ABOVE: John Strachey, Eddy's London flatmate, 1924.

RIGHT: Image of a dancing girl, from Eddy Sackville-West's personal collection at Knole.

In alcove in a dining-room painted on paper with deep blue and pale grey "écriture" and a yellow ochre border. The painted sideboard by Duncan Grant is in red, buff and apple green

A fireplace by Duncan Grant has a painted decoration of arum lilies and leaves in whites, greens and yellows, on a background of dull broken crimson. The tiles are also by Duncan Grant

A chair designed by Duncan Grant has a motif of grey vase and pear between emerald green curtains. It is worked in cross-stitch

This carpet, designed by Vanessa Bell, is in several shades of reds and browns and beige-pink

Another needle-work chair by Duncan Grant has a design of sky blue arum lilies and a border of turquoise circles on pink

and Vanessa Bell during the last few years, since the war. They can turn their versatile hands to anything, from the complete scheme of decoration down to the last detail of a drawing-room, to the painting of a bowl, a tile, a screen or a cushion, the designing of a carpet or a chair-cover. The pictures on the first page show panels painted in a room in the Tavistock Square house of Virginia Woolf, the brilliant author of *Jacob's Room* and *The Voyage Out*. The walls are a cool dove grey ; the borders of the panels are tomato-red, while the panels themselves are a glossy white. The oval *fonds* are alternately maple yellow and sienna pink, and the subjects are painted directly on to them in umbers, whites, and browns, with touches of lettuce green—a very cool, restful, and at the same time lively, scheme. Some of these panels were painted by Duncan Grant, some by Mrs. Bell. The narrow frieze round the top of the wall is in an amusing wall-paper, made simply by an *écriture* of brush-strokes in subdued violet on a white and lemon yellow ground. A wall-paper of the same kind was used in a dining-room alcove in a small house in Bloomsbury (shown in the top left-hand picture above), except in that this case the *écriture* is of deep blue and pale grey, bespattered with red spots, (Continued on page 106)

LEFT: Duncan Grant & Vanessa Bell's decorative schemes for Eddy's friend Angus Davidson at 3 Heathcote Street, Bloomsbury. Illustrated in *Vogue*, November 1924.

on the best teacups ... Sweets and jams stuck to his behind.' Leonard had to 'dust him, and pat him, and finally leave him; trying I believe, to smoke a pipe in full evening dress, and white waistcoat. They work very hard, the aristocracy.'

Eddy's own first novel, *Piano Quintet*, was also published in 1925. It was in this year that he was invited to join the Cranium Club, co-founded by Bunny Garnett and Stephen Tomlin. This monthly dining club met at Duncan Grant's spacious studio, placing Eddy at the heart of a buzzing literary and artistic community. Duncan Grant and Vanessa Bell were at the height of their popularity as decorative artists, producing brightly coloured schemes for the London flats of Eddy's friends Raymond Mortimer and Angus Davidson. Eddy flitted in and out of both these spaces, and would have seen them proudly illustrated in *Vogue*. In a *Vogue* review of 1924 Mortimer captured the transgressive spirit of the moment: 'The elderly say the country is decadent and going to the dogs ... it merely means that their own faculties are decaying and that they are going to the dogs themselves. Really the time in which we live is wildly interesting, fantastically romantic ... We are discarding our prejudices, each month sees the disappearance of some once formidable taboo.'

RIGHT: *Piano Quintet*, Eddy Sackville-West's first novel, published in 1925.

Stephen Tomlin and Duncan Grant

1925–1926

Eddy's artistic education became more intensely personal in 1925 when he embarked on a relationship with Stephen Tomlin. Known affectionately as Tommy, the sculptor had dropped out of Oxford to learn his craft with Frank Dobson. He was soon busy with commissions for portrait busts from his many friends in Bloomsbury. According to Frances Partridge, 'He had the striking profile of a Roman emperor on a coin, fair straight hair brushed back from a fine forehead, a pale face and grey eyes.' Handsome and dominant, he became an object of fascination for many.

Tommy, who was equally attracted to men and women, was not an easy person to love. His wife, Julia Strachey, suffered along with the rest: 'One thing was paramount: Tommy's daemon insisted that not only with their souls but definitely with their *bodies* everyone must him worship. This was the symbol and pledge of allegiance and subjection. And lo and behold, by the end of any party, everybody present – man, woman and child – had fallen in love with him ... those persons who hadn't been well and truly "laid" by him on previous occasions, and had their scalps duly collected, must be laid now at this party ... Maybe round a twisted corner of the terrace. Maybe indoors, up in the bathroom for instance.'

By January 1926 Eddy was worn out with unhappiness and despair, and went to recover, first in a nursing home, and then with his cousin Vita. Writing to her husband, Harold, Vita described how Eddy 'limped into my room, wasted away to a ghost and limped out again, back to bed. He had had a visit from the devastating Tomlin'.

Having reached the depths at New Year, Eddy sought solace in spring 1926 with Tommy's gentle former lover, Duncan Grant. Tommy produced a bronze portrait bust of Eddy, which perfectly captured his distinctive domed forehead and heavy lidded eyes. Eddy also acquired the original clay model for Tommy's 1924 sculpture of Duncan Grant. Both heads were displayed in Eddy's new apartment at Knole, forming an intriguing sculptural record of the relationships between a young writer and two erratic artists.

ABOVE: Stephen Tomlin working in his studio, photographed by John Banting, 1926.

RIGHT: Eddy's photograph of his lover Stephen Tomlin, c1925–6.

ABOVE: Duncan Grant, lover of Stephen Tomlin and Eddy Sackville-West, photographed by Alvin Langdon Coburn.

LEFT: Bust of Duncan Grant by Stephen Tomlin, 1924, acquired by Eddy Sackville-West for his rooms at Knole.

RIGHT: Portrait of Stephen Tomlin by John Banting, 1925.

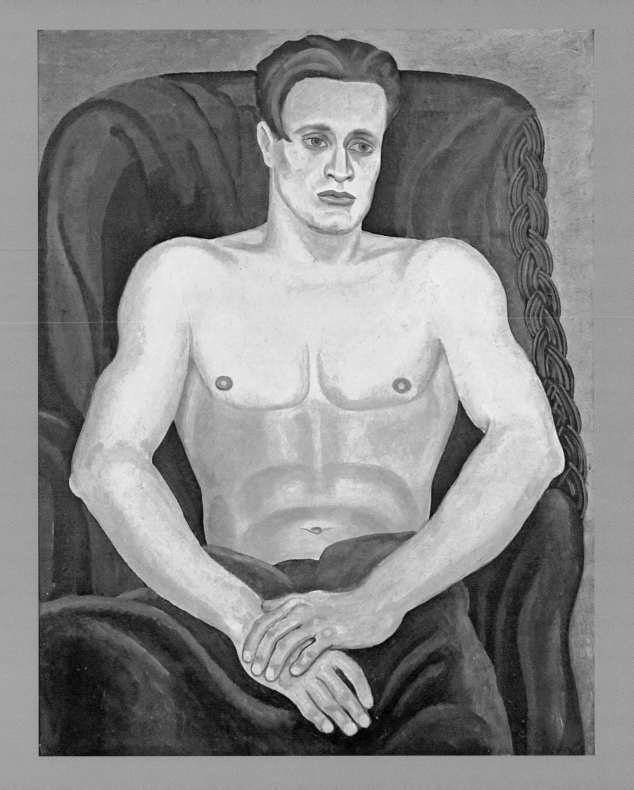

Decorating the Gatehouse Tower
January to May 1926

January 1926 marked a turning point in Eddy's life. Lord Sackville's unexpected offer of the suite of rooms at Knole gave him a new sense of purpose, and a new outlet for his creative energy. One moment he was lying in flat despair in a nursing home, brooding on his rejection by Stephen Tomlin; a week later he was making excited plans for the future, distracting Vita as she prepared for her journey to Tehran. Writing to Virginia Woolf she described 'Eddy chattering away while I try to pack. "Do you know Tom Eliot?" "No I don't." "Kodak films, aspirin, fur gloves, tooth powder." "Aren't the woodcuts in the Anatomy of Melancholy too lovely?" "No, Eddy, I think they're quite awful. Don't put my riding boots in my suitcase, one doesn't ride on board ship." "Shall I have my sitting room pink or yellow?" And so on.'

This snapshot of conversation gives a window into Eddy's busy mind. Knole presented him with the opportunity to crystallise all the artistic influences he had absorbed in Oxford and London: 1890s decadence, 1920s modernism, and the sexual inclusiveness of Bloomsbury. Faced with creating a suitably impressive decorative scheme for the Gatehouse Tower, colours became the immediate priority. The choice of pink for the main sitting room – soon renamed the Music Room – was deeply personal. This was the colour he had chosen as the backdrop for his 1920 portrait, signalling the 'cult of the effeminate' embraced by his Oxford contemporaries. And it appears again, paired dramatically with powder blue, in the strikingly androgynous Russell Flint image (see page 32) that Eddy preserved in his personal collection at Knole. Lipstick in hand, the sexually ambiguous figure gazes lovingly into a reflecting mirror.

ABOVE: The Gatehouse Tower at Knole.

RIGHT: Eddy's Music Room at Knole, with its distinctive pink and blue colour scheme, and fire screen painted by Duncan Grant.

ABOVE: The Deep Blue Turret Room – opening from the Music Room.

LEFT: From Eddy's personal collection at Knole: image of an androgynous figure applying lipstick, by Russell Flint.

This image, surely used as an inspiration for the Music Room, perfectly expresses Eddy's passion for feminine adornment. Virginia Woolf's letters are littered with references to Eddy's 'powder and paint', while Vita Sackville-West describes him as 'heavily made up', with 'a great gold bracelet on one wrist, and two gold rings'. Eddy's diaries dwell lovingly on his mother's dresses – 'a perfectly heavenly new evening-gown, champagne satin', and his own wardrobe – 'beautiful taffeta shirts with black stripe'. When the equally dapper Sitwell brothers, Osbert and Sacheverell, chose pink for their Chelsea drawing room in 1924, *Vogue* deliberately described it as

'Marie Laurencin pink' in honour of the bisexual French artist. Small wonder that Lytton Strachey, visiting Eddy at Knole in August 1926, described his apartments as 'ladylike'.

Eddy's personal collection at Knole contains a second androgynous image, which links closely to the colour scheme for his bedroom. Two intently gazing figures are set against a deep red backdrop, dressed in ornate flowered capes of iridescent blue. The scene conjures up Eddy's descriptions of nights in Vienna and Berlin: 'I was dragged about at night from one homosexual bar to another. The

behaviour is perfectly open. There are even large dance places for inverts. And some of the people one sees – huge men with breasts like women and faces like Ottoline, dressed as female Spanish dancers, are really quite unintelligible.' Sometimes the dragging was literal – one lover led him through the streets on a dog lead – 'I nearly expired with ecstasy'.

It is tempting to see the guiding hand of Duncan Grant in the palette Eddy selected for the remaining rooms at Knole: sage green for the staircases, lobbies and Dining Room; bedrooms in dark blue and mustard yellow; turret rooms of deep blue and pale green. Duncan often helped friends by prescribing the mixture of powder tints needed for their distempers, and the original pigments at Knole are very similar to those used at Charleston. Duncan may also have had a hand in the blue and gold astrological ceiling which once graced the Music Room, and the survival of a mysterious male figure drawn directly on the plaster hints at the consideration of more ambitious wall paintings.

The work programme for the Gatehouse Tower (January to May 1926) exactly matches the early months of their relationship. Duncan wrote to Bunny Garnett in April, urging secrecy – 'do not tell a soul I'm in love' – and in July he came to stay at Knole. A touching note written the following day to 'Dearest Eddy' begins: 'You must

ABOVE: 'Marie Laurencin pink' – favoured by both Eddy and the Sitwell brothers, and appearing here in Laurencin's portrait of Madame Paule Guillaume, c1924–8.

ABOVE LEFT: The Pale Green Turret Room, with the pink walls of the Music Room in the foreground.

know how happy I was at Knole, so it is rather absurd to tell you'; in August he declared, 'I think of you every day'. By September they were sharing titillating accounts of other liaisons: 'What have you done, what wickedness ... has brought upon you such exquisite sufferings? However, I am quite sure that with your sentries, and your chauffeurs, and your lighthouse keepers, and your scraping footboys, you are rather enjoying yourself. How I look forward to seeing you and twitting you face to face.'

ABOVE: From Eddy's personal collection at Knole: Image of two 'ladies' in red with deep blue capes.

RIGHT: Eddy Sackville-West's bedroom at Knole.

ABOVE: The fire surround in Eddy's bedroom, picked out in pink and blue.

TOP: Eddy's bedside table.

RIGHT: Eddy's Pink Turret Bathroom.

Furnishing the Gatehouse Tower

Although we may never know for sure exactly how much Duncan contributed to the decoration of the Gatehouse Tower, we can trace the works of art he produced for Eddy. A vibrant fire screen, with curling pink and blue flames, filled the arched stone fireplace in the Music Room. Even more distinctively, a series of Duncan's male nudes once hung on the same wall. A provocative feature in any home pre 1967, they were certainly striking enough to catch the eye of Mary Bates, secretary to the conductor Malcolm Sargent, who occupied Eddy's rooms during the Second World War. Lord Fairhaven of Anglesey Abbey, who started collecting male nudes by William Etty at a similar time, kept them carefully corralled in a bedroom corridor.

In 1928 Eddy commissioned a portrait from Grant that seems specially designed for the Music Room. It shows Eddy seated at the piano in Duncan's Fitzroy Square studio, his pale blue shirt contrasting with the pink floral wallpaper behind. Eddy had been renowned in his family as a child prodigy, who could play Chopin, Brahms and Wagner by ear. 'Long before I learnt to read novels, or even to enjoy verse read aloud to me, I was entirely familiar with the poetical transformation of musical sound. So natural to me was this process of transformation that the world of objects only became known to me in this way.' Music criticism was to form a key part of Eddy's later journalistic career, and his 1926 Steinway baby grand piano took a central place at Knole. Lytton Strachey remembered hearing 'quantities of music, both on piano and gramophone, interrupted from time to time, rather characteristically I thought, by a cuckoo-clock!'

ABOVE: Portrait of Eddy playing the piano by Duncan Grant, 1928.

RIGHT: A male nude by Duncan Grant; this painting hung at Eddy's later home, Long Crichel, and is now in the Radev Collection.

ABOVE: Eddy seated in the Music Room, 1927, photographed by John Banting.

Lytton's tongue-in-cheek description hints at another key feature of Eddy's rooms: humour. It was not just the passion for 'Marie Laurencin pink' that Eddy shared with Osbert and Sacheverell Sitwell. *Vogue*'s 1924 article on the Sitwells' Chelsea home flagged other characteristics: 'There are two ways of furnishing a house, the grimly historical, and the purely whimsical ... For now nothing will be in a room for any reason save that it amused the owner the day he put it there. It is his character, not his possessions, that gives the room its quality. Hence, if his character be sufficiently amusing his room will also be lovable.'

Eddy certainly made whimsical choices from the Knole heirlooms. In addition to the cuckoo-clock, he selected circular tapestry floor cushions, ornate Charles II winged chairs, witches' globes, plus the skulls and rapiers decried by Vita. As a host, he could certainly be lovable. Maurice Bowra described him as a 'frail elegant little figure', with 'an indomitable will that refused to admit defeat, and he countered his blackest hours with a delicious sense of fun and a ringing laugh'. This stood him in good stead when tackled by guests like the redoubtable lesbian composer, Ethel Smyth, who greeted him loudly at Sevenoaks station: 'Now then, Eddy, there are two things I want to talk to you about at Knole. One's the gramophone. The other is homosexuality.'

Eddy had created the perfect surroundings for queer conversation. His visitors' book, which opens in May 1926, reveals a skilful blend of handsome young contemporaries and the luminaries of Bloomsbury. As well as Lytton Strachey, Duncan Grant and Stephen Tomlin, Eddy entertained Bunny Garnett, Ralph Partridge, Desmond MacCarthy, E.M. Forster, L.P. Hartley, James and Alix Strachey, Raymond Mortimer, Angus Davidson, and Barbara Bagenal. Virginia Woolf lived close enough for regular visits; in 1926 she wrote to Vita: 'I like Eddy: I like the sharpness of his spine; his odd individualities and angles. But the young are dangerous. They mind so much what one thinks of them. One has to be very careful what one says.'

UNITY
IN
DIVERSITY

The House of Mr. Osbert

And Mr. Sacheverell Sitwell

THERE are two ways of furnishing a house, the grimly historical and the purely whimsical. We are all acquainted with the first style of furnishing, as we live in a pedantically historical age. Thus the cultured house-owner decides he wants his room to be, say, 1680, and everything in the room must belong absolutely to the year in question. Walnut furniture is placed elegantly in front of Mortlake tapestries, which are flanked by paintings after Lely. All the sofas are furnished with the same large green-and-black embroidery, complete with the Indian niggerboy to symbolise the first arrival of Asia. The visitor treads delicately between these harmonious masterpieces of a bygone age. Everything in the room is in period except the owner, and there is the snag in the system.

Very different is the whimsical method of decoration. For now nothing will be in a room for any reason, save that it amused the owner the day he put it there. It is his character, not his possessions, that gives the room its quality. Hence, if his character be sufficiently amusing his room will also be lovable. No. 2, Carlyle Square, the town house of Messrs. Osbert and Sacheverell Sitwell, is an excellent example of the whimsical style in furnishing. As we pass from the street into the hall, we enter apparently into the most unco-ordinated of worlds. Nothing in the house can be justified save on the all-important ground that it amused the Sitwells. Turning into the sitting-room on the left, we see such a collection of objects as can never have jostled elbows before. Half the pictures in the room might have been done to illustrate Mr. Sacheverell Sitwell's *Southern Baroque Art.* Here are some delightful drawings by Bibiena, the great theatrical designer of the eighteenth century, side by side with the neglected seventh-

Photographs by E. J. Mason

A fine ormolu Dolphin table, with brown marble top and gilded pedestal, occupies this corner in the back drawing-room of Mr. Sitwell's Chelsea house. Above, on a background of gorgeously shot gold brocade, hangs a little gallery of pictures by Severini. The sea-feeling inspired by the dolphin is strengthened by the shell-shaped chair beside it

Gargoyle heads from West Africa surmount the blue-framed mirrors, between the long windows which look out over the trees and grass of Carlyle Square. On the round table, covered with a wonderful piece of silken patchwork, the light falls through a magnificent piece of crimson Italian glass, whose modernity contrasts with the fine old blue Bristol which surrounds it

LEFT: Osbert and Sacheverell Sitwell's 'amusing' interiors, illustrated in *Vogue*, 1924. Like Eddy, they painted their Drawing Room in 'Marie Laurencin pink'.

John Banting

1927

In 1927 Eddy was seduced by a cheerfully disreputable artist who would have ignored Virginia Woolf's advice, and studiously refused to care what anybody said about him. John Banting provoked extreme reactions in almost everyone he met; Dolly Ponsonby called him 'one of the most evil-looking people I've ever set eyes on', while Clive Bell concluded after a dissolute summer in the South of France: 'It's a pity he thinks about nothing but drinking and fucking because I believe he has a talent – not for painting pictures, but for decorating. I shall be surprised if it comes to much.'

Bell's judgement seems a little harsh. Banting was a member of the London Group with a studio in Fitzroy Street, and had painted portraits of both Eddy and Stephen Tomlin in 1925. Later known for his surrealist work, Banting shared Eddy's defiance of convention and love of the absurd, and the joyful intensity of their relationship is captured in Banting's 1927 photograph album, now preserved in the Tate. Eddy found him 'congenial, interesting, good & beautiful', and invited him to Knole nine times between February and December 1927. They photographed each other in every possible pose: lying in hammocks, playing with statues, wearing Mexican sombreros, and staging mock executions. Banting took the only surviving image of Eddy in the Music Room, leaning back languidly in his Charles II chair, against a backdrop of books and lilies.

Flowers and stylised figures also feature in the artworks that Banting created for Eddy at Knole. On a corner cupboard, male and female nudes disport themselves amongst flowers and statues.

A tiny monochrome figure of the artist, brush in hand, emerges from a patch of brightly coloured lilies. On a screen, the naked torso and buttocks of a muscular baseball player balance a sensual image of a diver plunging into a lake. Equally playfully, Banting painted the box of Eddy's treasured E.M.G. gramophone with a jazz-age abstract pattern in deep blue, silver and black. Eddy's model is the Mark X, hand-made in the London factory for each client, with its distinctive cygnet shaped horn.

Although the initial intensity of their relationship had faded to friendship by 1928, the two men remained in touch for the rest of their lives. Banting included miniature portraits of Eddy and Raymond Mortimer amongst the 'tiny friends' painted on the loudspeaker of a radio at Ham Spray for Ralph and Frances Partridge. He introduced Eddy to the surrealist photographer Barbara Ker-Seymer, who photographed him against the backdrop of charging horses painted by Banting that decorated the walls of her studio above the jeweller Asprey on New Bond Street. Ker-Seymer's studio became a safe haven for many contemporaries who were exploring their sexuality or gender. Eddy's friend, the bisexual psychoanalyst Alix Strachey, succumbed to multiple representations: one of the most striking is a simple profile shot against the horse backdrop, which she sent to Eddy; others feature Alix in masculine mode, crop haired and leather jacketed, and in full surrealist gear, with giant rope and enigmatic silver cube.

RIGHT: Portrait of Eddy Sackville-West by John Banting, 1929.

ABOVE: John Banting's playful photo of Eddy in a sombrero, Knole, 1927.

ABOVE: John Banting with his dog, c1927.

ABOVE: John Banting climbing the stair to the Music Room at Knole, 1927.

Julia Strachey also sought refuge there after her marriage to Stephen Tomlin failed, and wrote to Frances Partridge with a delightful account of a typical few days with the Banting/Ker-Seymer coterie:

> *I discovered that Barbara had soon cheered up on the Saturday, and by teatime was wreathed around with Queens and supporters of all sorts, including the prime favourite – Lord Churchill. When I arrived on Sunday she was descried through a thick fog of tobacco smoke sitting on the knees of four Queens at once ... I had a crashing evening last night. John Banting invited his friend the 'genius hatter' back to Maddox Street, also Bryan Howard [sic.], Lord Churchill, Barbara and me, and by the light of two stump candles, completely in the nude, he flung himself over everything in a frenzied mating dance aimed at the genius.*

ABOVE: Eddy relaxing in a hammock at Knole, by John Banting, 1927.

RIGHT: Eddy's E.M.G. Gramophone, painted blue and silver by John Banting, 1927

ABOVE: Eddy's corner cupboard, painted with flowers and nude figures by John Banting, 1927.

ABOVE: John Banting painting the corner cupboard at Knole, 1927.

RIGHT: Stephen Tomlin (Tommy), John Banting, Julia Strachey and John Strachey, photographed by Barbara Ker-Seymer.

Decadent Moments

Although Banting loved naked dancing, he was equally fond of dressing up, and happily encouraged Eddy's more theatrical side. Vita Sackville-West may have curled her lip at Eddy's taste for velvet, swords, and coloured light bulbs, but he always remained loyal to his decadent roots. Eddy's passion for the macabre dated back to his Eton schooldays, when he had proudly compared himself to his friend Freddy Maxse: 'not being really a decadent, he thinks decadence a charming & amusing pose & adopts it, little knowing that he is playing with fire. He is proud of his decadent pose & flaunts decadence abroad. I, being really a decadent, am rather ashamed of it & try to overcome it & do not flaunt it more than I can help. Freddy's love of decadent art & literature will probably pass – mine certainly never will.'

Banting photographed Eddy reclining like Hamlet, gazing at a skull, and helped him to stage a mock execution, wielding a threatening axe. Skulls also appear in the Gothic bookplate designed for Eddy's library, inspired by *St Jerome in His Study*, a gloomy 1514 engraving by Albrecht Dürer which formed part of Eddy's collection. This plate depicts the distinctive arched windows in the **Gatehouse Tower,** and imagines his desk adorned with quills, a candlestick, an hourglass, a row of books, and cascading sheet music. There is also an impending sense of doom in the enigmatic turret rooms which open off the Music Room; one was known as the 'Nietzsche Room' in honour of the nihilistic creator of the 'master-slave' theory, with mysterious runes and part of the score of Busoni's *Doktor Faust* painted onto the wall.

Decadent themes abound in Eddy's Gothic novel *The Ruin*, which was published soon after he moved to Knole. The book was dedicated to his former lover, Adrian Stokes, and opens with a threatening quote from Friedrich Nietzsche: 'Are you a slave? Then you cannot be a friend. Are you a tyrant? Then you can have no friends.' As the story evolves, the human battle for domination between his characters is ultimately subservient to the rituals of the great house they inhabit; no one is strong enough to fight the 'mystical law of the house, which bade the keepers of its treasures utter the essential feelings of its own stage. The pictures – the countless pictures – the china, the carving, the silver, the gold, the furniture – all possessed a composite soul with which to rule their masters.'

Like his hero Joris-Karl Huysmans, the author of *À Rebours* (*Against Nature*), Eddy sought to combine theatricality with technical detail, morbid humour and subversive eroticism.

RIGHT: Eddy's 'decadent' bookplate, showing his desk in the Gatehouse Tower c1926, complete with skull, hourglass and guttering candle.

Ex Libris
Edward Sackville West

ABOVE: Eddy and John Banting stage a mock execution, Knole, 1927.

LEFT: The windowsill from Eddy's bedroom dressed with a skull and hourglass.

Eddy's hyperaesthesia, and his love of beautiful objects, comes through is in this highly charged description of two young men handling a jewelled box:

As he looked, Denzil saw beneath his face Marcus's hand come forward and touch the surface of the box with sensitive, caressing fingers. He saw how the nails grew from the flesh and compared their tarnished lustre with the agates' brilliancy. The middle finger-tip on the mineral, the index on the grey chaperone, the ring finger on the moonstone, they seemed to form a trio of new, unheard-of gems – a curious kind of agate, pink, flecked with tiny white clouds. He thought that the box might become set with finger-tips – some white, some pink. Then the hand moved and the fingers were laid lightly on the gilt chasing. The whole movement was replete with an animal grace and cunning that captivated Denzil. He seemed to feel those finger-tips upon his own face.

LEFT: Eddy's engraving of *St Jerome in his Study* by Albrecht Dürer – the inspiration for his 1926 bookplate.

LEFT: 'Decadent' landscape in the style of Gustave Moreau, bought by Eddy while he was at Oxford and now hanging in his bedroom at Knole.

LEFT: From the walls of the Blue Turret Room, known as the 'Nietzsche Room': score of *Doktor Faust* and runes, painted by John Banting, *c*1927.

Androgyny and the Bright Young Things

If Eddy was sensitive to the erotic charge of jewelled fingertips on a young man's face, he was equally alive to the possibilities of personal adornment. Decadents like Max Beerbohm had written whole treatises in defence of cosmetics, and Eddy was a passionate advocate of the art. Sometimes this was not for beauty's sake alone, but to hide the skin lesions caused by his hereditary telangiectasia, which could lead to agonising haemorrhages: 'Pain was personal to me, shared with no one else, an individual demon of intolerable beauty, with heart and hands that existed only as instruments by which I was kept for ever in this fiery suspension between the heaven of life and the viewless planet...'

Vita Sackville-West and Virginia Woolf clucked disapprovingly about Eddy's tendency to 'paint and powder', and the bewildering similarity of his young friends of either sex, dismissed by Virginia as 'tubular cropheads'. Vita described a party held at Knole for Eddy's sister in 1927 as being full of 'slim young creatures all looking as though they had come straight out of the *Tatler*, all indistinguishable one from another, and young men to match. They lay about on the grass, like aristocratic young animals with sleek heads. I was acutely conscious of the difference of generation'. In the same year, Eddy appeared in *Vogue*, snapped by Cecil Beaton with a cornucopia of 'Bright Young Things', lying upside down under a leopard skin. The scene took place at Wilsford, home of Siegfried Sassoon's androgynous lover, Stephen Tennant.

Tennant was an object of erotic fascination for Eddy's circle; Virginia Woolf recorded her sense of exclusion during an evening at Raymond Mortimer's when Eddy arrived late from the theatre, and a fetching

BELOW: 'A group of Intelligent Young Persons', Cecil Beaton's photograph taken at Wilsford for *Vogue*, 2 November 1927.

From left to right: Sacheverell Sitwell, Stephen Tennant, Rosamund Lehmann, Osbert Sitwell, Georgia Sitwell, Elinor Wylie, Cecil Beaton, Rex Whistler, Eddy Sackville-West, Zita Jungman.

photograph of Stephen 'in a tunic, in an attitude' was passed around the room: 'The other buggers pricked their ears & became somehow silly ... An atmosphere entirely secluded, intimate & set on one object: all agreed upon the things they liked ... This all made on me a tinkling, private, giggling impression. As if I had gone into a men's urinal.'

In July 1930 Eddy joined forces with Alix Strachey's girlfriend, Nancy Morris, to throw their famous 'Hermaphrodite Party'. Frances Partridge recorded how most of the young men had 'loaded themselves with pearls, powder and paint'. She found the atmosphere so stifling and the noise so deafening that 'even the music from a vast gramophone horn was inaudible'. And she picked up the inevitable hint of decadence in all of Eddy's creations, bemoaning the 'vogue now for such parties as this, all of the creative energy of the participants goes into their dress, and there are none of the elaborate performances of earlier parties. Personally I think this is a sad come-down, a sign of decadence.'

LEFT: 'Like father, like son' – caricature contrasting the musical Eddy with his soldier father, by Anthony Wysard, 1938.

RIGHT: Image of an androgynous figure in black ballet shoes, from Eddy's personal collection at Knole.

FAR RIGHT: Dorothy Wellesley (?), Clive Bell, Vita Sackville-West, and Eddy Sackville-West, playing tennis at Vita's house, Long Barn, 1927.

Farewell to Knole, 1939

As the 1930s progressed, Eddy continued to entertain friends and lovers at Knole, but he became increasingly embroiled in a tormenting affair with married MP, Paul Latham. Handsome and sadistic, Latham demanded complete subservience, which Eddy tried to provide: 'I feel an absolute compulsion to sacrifice myself to him – as far as that is possible – because in spite of everything he is *not* nothing – there is real character there, an interesting & fine one.' Thanks to Latham's political role, the relationship had to be carried out in complete secrecy, which left Eddy feeling increasingly lonely and depressed. By 1937 he was writing to Raymond Mortimer explaining that, 'I find it intolerable to have to reconcile myself to the prospect of living for ever alone.' In the same year, he told Molly MacCarthy, 'An independent income does not make life as long as Communists (and even Socialists) seem to imagine. The miseries are different, that is all.'

In August 1939 Virginia Woolf told Vita that she had received a visit from Eddy 'and really he wrung my heart'. She goes on to imply that he had thought of suicide. When war broke out in September 1939, Eddy sought friendly companionship elsewhere. He moved first to Upton, home of Sir Kenneth Clark, Director of the National Gallery, and then to West Wycombe, to live with the Dashwoods. The young couple had filled the house with a group of convivial lodgers, and it was here that Eddy made such a profound impression on novelist Nancy Mitford that she immortalised him in the character of hypochondriac Uncle Davey in *The Pursuit of Love*. Such was the cold in the house that Eddy attended each meal dressed in a deep blue velvet opera cloak, from beneath which he withdrew an array of jewelled snuff boxes. These

ABOVE: Eddy's image of his lover in the 1930s, Sir Paul Latham MP, by Dorothy Wilding, signed 'Paul, 1936'.

were laid out solemnly on the table before him, each containing a different pill for each of his current ailments.

Eddy's rooms at Knole were left untouched throughout the war, occupied first by his young cousin Ben Nicolson, and then by the conductor Malcolm Sargent. Ben's diary for September 1939 describes his excitement: 'I'm living in Eddy's spare room, using his sitting room in the Tower. It has always been my ambition to live here, with all the books in the world sitting on the shelves unread, asking to be read.'

Eddy never returned to live at Knole, preferring to set up a home with Raymond Mortimer, Desmond Shawe-Taylor and Eardley Knollys at Long Crichel in Dorset. But his watchful presence overlooked every subsequent inhabitant: in 1929 Eddy asked the artist Paul Hamann to create his life mask, which was mounted onto the wall of the spiral staircase, outside the Music Room. Cast in plaster, with eyes directed downwards, and each eyelash clearly rendered, it stands guard over Eddy's carefully constructed world.

ABOVE: Eddy Sackville-West by Bassano Ltd, June 1930.

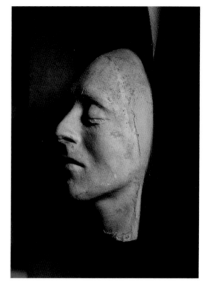

ABOVE: Bust of Eddy Sackville-West by Paul Hamann, 1929.

TOP: Eddy's life mask, made by Paul Hamann in Berlin 1929, and fitted to the entrance of the Music Room at Knole.

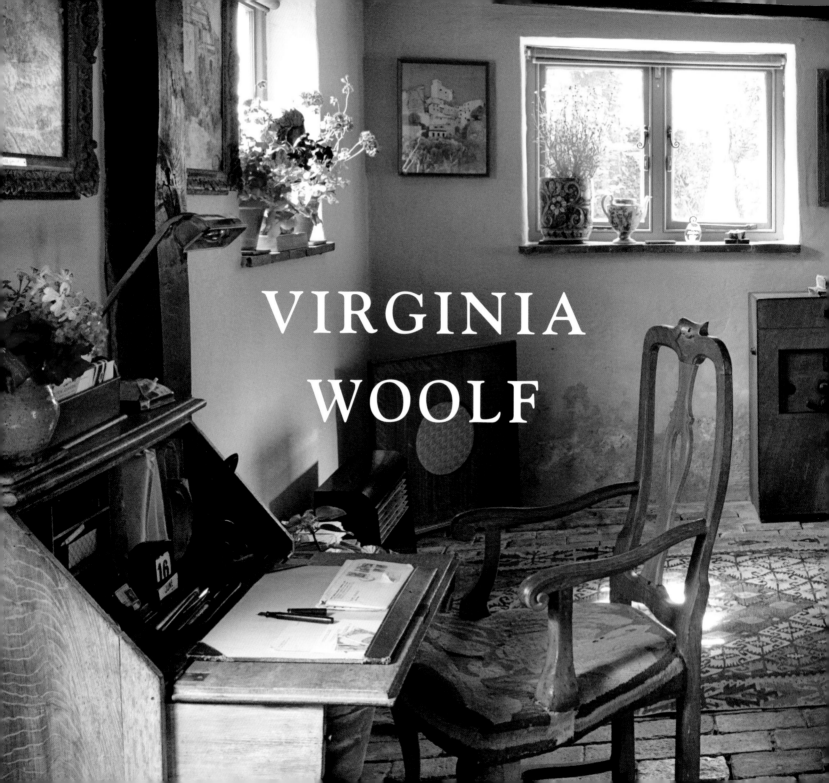

VIRGINIA WOOLF

Virginia's 'triumph', her 'combined drawing eating room' at Monk's House.

Virginia Woolf, Monk's House, 1928

Forty miles south of Knole, Virginia Woolf and her sister Vanessa Bell created Sussex homes at Monk's House and Charleston which embodied their commitment to a new way of living. The Bloomsbury Group celebrated sexual equality and freedom, feeling that every person had the right to live and love in the way that they chose. The two sisters both formed lasting relationships which stretched beyond heterosexual norms, adapting to embrace same-sex love for other partners. Both Monk's House and Charleston are filled with works of art produced by the queer cross-gender collaboration of Vanessa Bell and Duncan Grant. Their distinctive combination of bright colours, abstract patterns and eclectic objects gives a joyful feeling of comfort and informality. There is a sense that anything could happen and anything could be said in these Bloomsbury-inspired rooms – eroticism and humour are never far from the surface.

Monk's House is very different in scale to Eddy's apartment at Knole, but equally expressive of its owner's personality. Virginia poured every available penny of the money she earned from her books into the house, making 16 successive alterations between 1919 and 1941. Ably assisted by her husband Leonard and local builders Philcox Brothers, she arranged for walls to be knocked down, extensions built, bathrooms added. The 'queer, poky jumbled cottage' dismissed by Vanessa was gradually transformed into a 'desirable, roomy, light house'. By 1929 you could see from one end of the building to the other, opening up views to Virginia's 'large combined drawing eating room, with its 5 windows, its beams down the middle, & flowers & leaves nodding in all around us.' Here she indulged her passion for soft green walls and vibrant furniture in the style of the Omega Workshop – a design company founded for and by members of the Bloomsbury Group. These included lilac chairs picked out in yellow, powder blue and sage green by Vanessa; tables covered by Duncan with sensuous figurative tiles; chair seats designed by their daughter Angelica showing a full breasted Leda embracing the swan. Writing to thank Vanessa in 1929 she complained ironically 'Everyone who comes throws up their hands – says where do you get these lovely things? And I feel my gorges swell.'

The tiny cottage was soon filled with a bewildering array of Bloomsbury guests. John Lehmann, the publisher and poet, described the 'continual *va-et-vien*' between Monk's House and Charleston, and the stream of visitors who stayed for the night. Sitting by the fireside, long cigarette holder in hand, Virginia would encourage the open communication for which Bloomsbury was renowned. John Lehmann remembered how 'the conversation was apt to turn very soon to our mutual friends, their affairs and their *amours*. Virginia had an insatiable curiosity about their

RIGHT: Virginia Woolf, 1928.

ABOVE AND RIGHT: Virginia's 'combined drawing eating room', the site of many convivial gatherings.

sexual adventures, and a gift for drawing one out to be indiscreet. Nothing, I believe, could shock her, though some revelations I made surprised her, particularly about the way of life of friends like myself in London. Leonard, puffing at his pipe which was always going out, would nod his head sagely while I uncovered the hidden life that seemed so often news to Virginia – though news she triumphed in having drawn out. My retaliation was to make them both talk about the early life of Bloomsbury, the personalities, the interconnecting liaisons. It was sometimes quite late before we broke up for bed.'

ABOVE: T.S. Eliot taking tea in the
'combined drawing eating room'.

ABOVE: Foley teapot and matching cup in purple lustre,
yellow and gold, designed by Vanessa Bell, 1934.

ORLANDO

ORLANDO ON HER RETURN TO ENGLAND

By

VIRGINIA WOOLF

9s. net

Just Published by

THE HOGARTH PRESS, 52 TAVISTOCK SQUARE, W.C.1

This is not a sample of the printing
which is execrable.

DEDICATED
(BY PERMISSION)
TO THE
Honourable Mrs. HAROLD NICOLSON

or
to the
Honourable V. Sackville West

or
to the
Honourable Victoria Sackville West

or to Vita Nicolson

Printed in Great Britain by R. & R. Clark, Limited, Edinburgh.

Eddy, Vita, Virginia
1928

In October 1928 Virginia Woolf published *Orlando*, the book which would forever link her name with Vita Sackville-West. First meeting in 1922, their relationship reached a crescendo between 1924 and 1926, returning to friendship from 1927 as Vita's erotic focus moved on to others. Both women were married, so the physical canvas of their encounters can be traced across their respective marital homes. Writing from her Kent house, Long Barn, in October 1927, Vita declared to Virginia – 'how right I was ... to force myself on you at Richmond, and to lay the trail for the explosion which happened on the sofa in my room here when you behaved so disgracefully and acquired me for ever.' Virginia eagerly anticipated Vita's visits to Monk's House, and shared her excitement in letters to Vanessa: 'Vita is now arriving to spend 2 nights alone with me – L is going back. I say no more, as you are bored by Vita, bored by love, bored by me ... still the June nights are long and warm, the roses flowering, and the garden full of lust and bees.'

Although *Orlando* was written for Vita – 'it's all about you and the lusts of your flesh and the lure of your mind' – it was also a tribute to Knole, the house Vita loved but could not inherit; a building where 'silver shone and lacquer glowed and wood kindled; when the carved chairs held their arms out and dolphins swam apon the walls'. Orlando

LEFT: Press cuttings for *Orlando*, 1928, featuring the photograph of Vita taken in Duncan Grant's studio, used to illustrate 'Orlando on her return to England'.

lives for four centuries, changing sex, but retaining firm possession of his/her ancient home. One passage above all captures Virginia's sense of human connectivity to place: 'She, who believed in no immortality, could not help feeling that her soul would come and go forever with the reds on the panels and the greens on the sofa. For the room ... shone like a shell that has lain at the bottom of the sea for centuries and has been crusted over and painted a million tints by the water; it was rose and yellow, green and sand-coloured. It was frail as a shell, as iridescent and as empty ... Gently opening a door, she stood on the threshold so that (as she fancied) the room could not see her and watched the tapestry rising and falling on the eternal faint breeze which never failed to move it. Still the hunter rode; still Daphne flew. The heart still beat, she thought, however faintly, however far withdrawn; the frail indomitable heart of the immense building.'

Inheritance, sexuality and gender were live issues at Knole in 1928, and Virginia tackled all three subjects in *Orlando*. Vita's father died in January 1928, pushing her first cousin Eddy firmly into the spotlight as the male heir. The deliciously comic irony of this situation appealed to Virginia, who was very aware that the 'love-making' which Eddy carried out so openly in the Gatehouse Tower would never produce any 'child-bearing'. While Eddy was a model of delicate femininity, happily mincing in black velvet in his ladylike apartments, Vita dressed in breeches, adopting the alter ego of 'Julian' when she eloped with Violet Trefusis. Virginia's diaries and letters reveal her delight in

ABOVE: Image of Vita from *Orlando*, used to illustrate 'Orlando at the present time'. Taken by Leonard Woolf.

LEFT: Virginia Woolf, photographed and described by Vita at Knole, 1928: 'We wandered all over the house yesterday, pulling up the blinds, she was thrilled. She and Dad got on splendidly.'

ABOVE: Virginia and Vita sitting in the garden at Monk's House, August 1933. Taken by Leonard Woolf.

ABOVE: Vita's gift to Virginia: a piece of bright blue Persian pottery from her journey to Tehran, 1926. The rest of the set is displayed in her Writing Room at Sissinghurst.

pumping both cousins for erotic gossip, and in *Orlando* she produced 'a whole fantasy ... Sapphism is to be suggested. Satire is to be the main note – satire & wildness ... an escapade after these serious poetic experimental books whose form is always so closely considered'.

Although Virginia had been in love with Vita, she was fascinated by Eddy, and sensitive to his fears of legal exposure. In May 1928 she wrote to her sister Vanessa: 'Then there's Eddy back and as prickly as a hedgehog. Old Lady Sackville is bringing a case against his father, which will mean that all their characters will be blackened in the Law Courts – Already she has scattered it broadcast that Harold's a bugger, and Vita a sapphist. This upsets Eddy considerably; but he was rather nice, queer, acid, prickly and immensely sorry for himself.' Eddy was right to be worried; Radclyffe Hall's explicit lesbian novel *The Well of Loneliness* caused a public backlash in July 1928, with the *Sunday Express* leading a campaign for suppression on moral grounds. The editor, James Douglas, claimed that 'sexual inversion and perversion' had become too visible, and society needed to 'cleanse itself from the leprosy of these lepers'.

Despite the best efforts of Virginia Woolf, E.M. Forster and a host of contemporary writers who offered to give evidence for the defence, Radclyffe Hall's book was banned for obscenity in November 1928. Although *Orlando*'s century-hopping storyline was too wildly fanciful to attract the attention of the Home Secretary, it gives a clear indication of Virginia's increasingly open approach to sexuality and human desire, and a sense of the conversations she encouraged at Monk's House between her gay friends. Writing in 1930 to the lesbian composer Ethel Smyth, she wryly refers to a longstanding debate with Eddy: 'When I go to what we call a Buggery Poke party, I feel as if I had strayed into the male urinal; a wet, smelly, trivial kind of place. I fought with Eddy Sackville over this; I often fight with my friends. How silly, how pretty you sodomites are I said; whereat he flared up and accused me of having a red-nosed grandfather.'

In the same letter, Virginia concludes: 'Where people mistake, as I think, is in perpetually narrowing and naming these immensely composite and wide flung passions – driving stakes through them, herding them between screens. But how do you define 'Perversity'? What is the line between friendship and perversion?' Here she was going much further than contemporary sexologists like Havelock Ellis, who regarded homosexuality as an inborn and inalterable trait, defined as 'congenital sexual inversion'. In *Orlando*, her hero triumphantly evades such categorisations, changing their sexuality and gender over time. Putting aside the teasing language of her private exchanges with Eddy and Vita, Virginia introduces universal concepts which we would describe today as gender-fluid and pansexual:

Different though the sexes are, they intermix. In every human being a vacillation from one sex to the other takes place and often it is only the clothes that keep the male or female likeness, while underneath the sex is the very opposite of what it is above. Of the complications and confusions which thus result everyone has had experience. But here we leave the general question and note only the odd effect that it had in the particular case of Orlando herself. For it was this mixture in her of man and woman, one being uppermost and then the other, that often gave her conduct an unexpected turn.

RIGHT: Portrait of Radclyffe Hall, author of *The Well of Loneliness*.

Monk's House – a 'comfortable, charming, characteristic, queer resort'

Virginia Woolf, 1926

Virginia's love for Monk's House was as strong as Vita's for Knole. She loved the long, rambling nature of the modest 18th-century cottage, boarded on one side, brick and flint on the other: 'There is little ceremony or precision at Monk's House. It is an unpretending house, long & low, a house of many doors.' Within hours of Leonard's successful bid at auction in July 1919 she was confidently asserting: 'Monk's House ... will be our address for ever and ever. Indeed, I've already marked out our graves in the yard which joins our meadow.' And she quickly formed romantic associations with previous owners, buying primitive portraits of the Glazebrook family who had lived in the house in the 19th century: 'For myself, I don't ask anything more of pictures. They are family groups, and he began the heads very large, and hadn't got room for the hands and legs, so these dwindle off till they're about the size of sparrows claws, but the effect is superb – the character overwhelming.'

Other visitors were quick to pick up on the quirky charm; built into the hillside, water tended to pour down the precipitous entrance stair along with the guests. Angelica Garnett described how 'one stepped into it, rather as though one steps into a boat'. John Lehmann noticed how the house seemed to have 'grown by itself in a shambling way; no overall plan to it, with short, worn, staircases appearing in unexpected places'. Stephen Spender admired the plants which 'knocked at the small-paned windows as though longing to come in', making the rooms feel cool on the warmest day, and giving a feeling of being underwater.

ABOVE: Monk's House – the modest boarded exterior, facing the village street.

ABOVE: Monk's House – view from end to end, with 'staircases appearing in unexpected places'.

Creating alteration after alteration, Virginia bravely adapted this unlikely receptacle into a vessel for post-impressionist art and the legacy of the Omega Workshops.

Undeterred by Vita, who found Vanessa and Duncan's paintings 'of inconceivable hideousness', Virginia stuck to her Bloomsbury artistic roots. Back in 1904, she and her sister had joyfully abandoned the dark Victorian rooms of their childhood home in Hyde Park Gate, entering a new era of light and colour at 46 Gordon Square. This move to Bloomsbury signalled the start of a different way of living.

ABOVE: Monk's House – the steps down into the house from the garden.

ABOVE: The Dining Room mantel, with the primitive portrait of the Glazebrook family (former owners) hanging above.

LEFT: View of the open plan Dining Room, hung with paintings by Vanessa Bell and Roger Fry.

FAR LEFT: On the opposite wall, Vanessa Bell's portrait of Virginia, 1912, hangs above a music cabinet decorated by Grant and Bell in 1932.

to revolutionise our knowledge of our own minds and of the universe. Equally exciting things were happening in the arts ... In painting we were in the middle of the profound revolution of Cezanne, Matisse and Picasso ... And to crown it all, night after night, we flocked to Covent Garden, entranced by a new art, a revolution to us benighted British, the Russian Ballet in the greatest days of Diaghilev and Nijinsky.'

Virginia described their plans 'to paint; to write; to have coffee after dinner instead of tea'. Vanessa remembered the sense of freedom – 'We did not hesitate to talk of anything ... You could say what you liked about art, sex or religion.'

Surrounded by a like-minded circle of friends, the sisters connected to the mood of the moment. In the words of Leonard Woolf:

'The revolution of the motor car and the aeroplane had begun. Freud and Rutherford and Einstein were at work beginning

Virginia was an enthusiastic supporter of the post-impressionist exhibitions mounted by her friend Roger Fry, and the London Group of artists associated with Vanessa and Duncan. Although she bought works by Roger Fry, Duncan Grant and Frederick Porter, her main focus was inevitably Vanessa. She wrote introductions to catalogues, funded opening-night parties, and acquired paintings whenever money was available. Vanessa also became the most prolific artist to work for the Hogarth Press, designing the wolf's head colophon, as well as countless covers for Virginia's books. And when Vanessa and Duncan decided to set up a house-decorating practice from Duncan's Fitzroy Street studio in 1922, Virginia was determined to give them a commission.

ABOVE: Vanessa Bell's yellow Cezanne-style *Apples*, 1919 (Dining Room).

ABOVE: Vanessa Bell's red abstract *Bottles on a Table*, 1915 (Dining Room).

LEFT: An array of painted trays in the kitchen, including a vivid image of a 'May Queen' raising her hands.

FAR LEFT (TOP): Roger Fry's *Landscape at Asheham*, 1913 (Dining Room).

BELOW: Duncan Grant's *Reclining Nude*, 1919.

Bloomsbury in Vogue

In January 1924 Virginia and Leonard decided to sell their house in Richmond, and buy a ten-year lease of 52 Tavistock Square, Bloomsbury. They installed the Hogarth Press in the basement, let the ground and first floors to solicitors, and moved into the top two floors themselves: 'L. and I on top looking at all the glories of London, which are romantically, sentimentally, incredibly dear to me.' Here was the perfect space to experiment with a bold artistic statement, and soon Virginia's rooms were filled with 'vast panels of moonrises and prima donnas' bouquets – the work of Vanessa and Duncan Grant'.

Author William Plomer felt the murals gave 'a contribution to the unsolemn atmosphere of a room not quite like any other'. Virginia chose the soft green tones she favoured at Monk's House, and *Vogue* was full of praise for the results: 'a very cool, restful, and at the same time lively scheme'. The large figurative panels featured books and musical instruments, and were painted in 'umbers, browns and white, with touches of lettuce green'; the walls were 'pale dove grey' with 'tomato-red **borders**', with a cornice frieze of 'subdued violet on white and lemon yellow'.

Virginia particularly admired the fireplace, which Vanessa painted in 'a tender blue, like the blue of a chalk hill blue, or the sea at a distance, with chalk cliffs in the foreground'. Against this stood a fire screen designed by Duncan, showing flowers and a lute against a delicate seascape. Eddy Sackville-West lent the Woolfs his piano, and the

rooms became the springboard for Virginia's re-entry to London life: 'music, talk, friendship, city views, books, publishing, something central and inexplicable, all this is now within my reach'. This was the peak point for transgressive Bloomsbury parties, and Virginia happily joined the throng. Vanessa remembered her sister dressing as Sappho for 'one of those parties where the ladies dress as men and vice versa', and the confusing experience of finding herself ardently pursued by a gentleman who was convinced that she was a man in drag.

Tavistock Square was not the only Bloomsbury interior to feature in *Vogue* in 1924. From 1922 to 1926 *Vogue* was edited by the masterful Dorothy Todd, ably assisted by her partner, fashion editor Madge Garland. Rebecca West called Madge and Dody 'two very remarkable women' who 'changed *Vogue* from just another fashion paper to being the best of the fashion papers and a guide to the modern movement in the arts'. In Lisa Cohen's view they created a magazine which represented 'the English and French avant-garde as a fashionable world', seeing 'haute couture, painting ... photography, literature,' and interior design as part of the same expression of modernity.

Soon articles by Virginia Woolf or Vita Sackville-West were appearing alongside Cecil Beaton photographs and features on Grant and Bell interiors. Madge Garland was an early patron of Beaton, and by a strange twist of fate the first of his images that she selected for *Vogue* depicted someone very well known to the Woolfs: their handsome young assistant at Hogarth Press, Geroge 'Dadie' Rylands,

Panels by Duncan Grant and Vanessa Bell in Mrs. Woolf's house in Tavistock Square. The walls are pale dove-grey, the panels glossy white with tomato-red borders and oval "fonds" alternately in sienna pink and maple yellow. The subjects are painted in umbers, browns, and white, with touches of lettuce-green. The narrow frieze is in wallpaper with "écriture" of subdued violet on white and lemon yellow

MODERN ENGLISH DECORATION

Some Examples of the Interesting Work

Of Duncan Grant and Vanessa Bell

Three panels in detail, from the room illustrated above

FOR some time past " period " rooms have been the fashion. First it was the picturesque Elizabethan and Jacobean, then Queen Anne, the eighteenth century, the Regency, the French " Empire," and even, latterly, the Victorian. Very charming such rooms can be, with their pleasant literary associations, their slight air of " pose." But, necessarily, they are a little artificial, in that they are the products of a bygone age, whose thoughts, whose aspirations, whose whole life was totally different from ours. But is there any reason why we should not consider our own day as a " period "—the only period for us which is not in some sense artificial—and set aside at any rate one room in our own house which shall be truly representative of the best in it ? It is not as if this were an age devoid of artistic effort ; on the contrary, there is at present in this country an artistic activity which is producing work more interesting and more vital than anything that has made its appearance here during the last hundred years. Moreover,

many of the leading artists in this modern movement (which is derived largely from Cézanne and the French Impressionists, though it must not for a moment be supposed, as some critics have suggested, that it despises the Old Masters) have turned their attention to decorative work.

Among these are Duncan Grant and Vanessa Bell, who even before the war were associated with a group of artists who produced work of this kind under the leadership of Roger Fry. The war, unfortunately, put a complete stop to this enterprise, but not before they had produced a great many charming things in the way of furniture, stuffs, and pottery, practical as well as beautiful. The individual practical aspect of each object is one of the things to which the artist decorator pays the greatest attention. In the useful arts, beauty and usefulness are interdependent, and mere ornament which hinders practical use is, *ipso facto*, inartistic.

The illustrations to this article are all taken from decorative work done by Duncan Grant

RIGHT: 'Modern English Decoration', *Vogue* 1924. Duncan Grant and Vanessa Bell's murals for Virginia Woolf at 52 Tavistock Square, Bloomsbury. These featured the soft green tones she also favoured at Monk's House.

ABOVE: Virginia photographed in Tavistock Square in 1939, with the soft greens and greys of the murals in the background.

ABOVE: Vanessa Bell's portrait of Virginia at Tavistock Square, 1934.

dressed as the Duchess of Malfi. Madge was equally captivated by Virginia's haunting looks – 'I saw a very beautiful woman ... she had an angular face, high cheek-bones, deep-set eyes, an almost Madonna-like appearance' – and longed to put 'all that beauty into its right setting'.

In 1926 she got her chance. Early that year Cecil Beaton noticed Madge 'looking perfect in a most lovely costume by Nicole Groult. Very influenced by Marie Laurencin – in pale blue and pink'. Parisian fashion designer Groult was an intimate friend of French artist Marie Laurencin, described in *Vogue* as 'a sister of Sappho' whose art displayed 'a sort of wittiness mixed with wantonness. She will emphasize a pout, an attitude, an expression, a gesture, as character, which is witty; and also as a perverse physical attraction, which is wanton. The spectator is continually being reminded of the peculiar perverse desirability of women.'

Virginia Woolf admired the outfit so greatly that Madge arranged to have it copied in Paris, asking Nicole to do a personal fitting when she was over for her London show. Virginia's version was blue rather than pink, and featured the same 'long silk coat of a plain colour, lined with the pattern, and beautifully bordered'. The outcome was eye-catching, causing Lady Ottoline Morrell to take 16 successive photographs of Virginia from every angle when she wore it to Garsington that summer. And it provided the perfect setting for what Christopher Isherwood described as 'those wonderful, forlorn eyes; the slim, erect, high-shouldered figure ... the hair folded back from the eggshell fragility of the temples; the small, beautifully cut face'.

1926 proved a sad turning point for *Vogue*; with circulation figures dwindling, Condé Nast fired first Dody, then Madge, hinting at an exposure of their 'morals' if they tried to sue. The affair quickly became a talking point in Bloomsbury. Virginia Woolf reported to Vanessa Bell: 'It is said that Conde Nast threatened to reveal Todds [sic] private sins, if she sued them, so she is taking £1000 and does not bring an action.' Vita Sackville-West concluded ruefully that 'poor Todd is silenced, since her morals are of the classic rather than the conventional order'.

RIGHT: Duncan Grant's embroidered fire screen for Tavistock Square, now at Monk's House.

Virginia's admirer, *Vogue*
fashion editor Madge
Garland, photographed
by Cecil Beaton, 1927.

ABOVE: Virginia's handsome assistant at the Hogarth Press, George 'Dadie' Rylands, dressed as the Duchess of Malfi. Cecil Beaton's photograph of Dadie as the Duchess was his first to be published in *Vogue*.

RIGHT: Virginia wearing the beautiful blue Nicole Groult dress procured for her by Madge Garland, Garsington Manor, June 1926. Madge owned the same dress in pink.

'The Display of one's own Character'
Virginia Woolf, 1927

Successive biographers have portrayed Virginia as tentative in her decorative and fashion choices, deferring to her artist sister in matters of design. They quote a self-deprecating letter to Vanessa of May 1927 – 'I have my own ideas and my own taste, but its [sic] all ineradicably bad' – and a diary entry where she feels mocked for her love of green paint. Despite these occasional lapses in confidence, Virginia seems remarkably decisive in her treatment of Monk's House. In particular, she was proud of her 'perfect triumph', the combined drawing and eating room created in 1926, where she presided over family tea parties, reducing her nephews to helpless laughter with her outrageous flights of fancy.

Returning from a visit to Vita in 1927, she records the simple joy of being back in this room, amongst her own distinctive things: 'Back from Long Barn ... Such opulence & freedom, flowers all out, butler, silver, dogs, biscuits, wine, hot water, log fires, Italian cabinets, Persian rugs, books ... Yet I like this room better, perhaps; more effort & life in it, to my mind, unless this is the prejudice one has naturally in favour of the display of one's own character.' For Virginia, possessions were powerful reflectors of personality, and a stimulus to her own creativity. Writing to Ethel Smyth in 1930 she declared 'You can't think what a shock of emotion it gives me – seeing people among their things – I've lots [sic] such scenes in my head; the whole of life presented – the other persons [sic] life – for 10 seconds; and then it goes; and comes again'.

Possessions could also be symbols of independence and free choice. Following the commercial success of *Orlando* in 1928, she joyfully recorded the excitement of spending money she had earned herself in exactly the way she wished: 'For the first time since I married 1912–28 – 16 years – I have been spending money ... All this money making originated in a spasm of black despair one night at Rodmell 2 years ago. I was tossing up & down on those awful waves: when I said I could find a way out.' Virginia felt stifled by 'the perpetual limitation of everything; no chairs, or beds, no comfort, no beauty; & no freedom to move.' This she determined to change, 'and so came, with some argument, even tears one night ... to an agreement with Leonard about sharing money after a certain sum.'

Money earned from her own books was soon combined with money earned from Vita, whose novels *The Edwardians* (1930) and *All Passion Spent* (1931) were best-sellers for the Hogarth Press. Some of this largesse was spent on bringing back furniture and ceramics from holidays in France. But more was set aside for direct commissions to Vanessa and Duncan: textiles printed with their designs by Allan Walton; pots thrown to their designs by Phyllis

RIGHT: Tile-topped coffee table commissioned by Virginia for Monk's House, featuring a sensuous 'Venus at her Toilet' in blue, yellow and sage green, Duncan Grant, 1930.

Keyes, and objects specially made for Monk's House, carefully chosen to contrast with the soft green walls of the sitting room.

Virginia wrote to 'Bell, Decorator' in 1929 asking for two tables – one painted, the other tiled – 'Have you got one of those tile tables? If so what price? Or could you make one?' The finished objects combine Grant's fanciful figures with Bell's circles, arcs and curves. Duncan's tile-topped coffee table features a resplendent 'Venus at her toilet', accompanied by a half-naked attendant playing the lute. Vanessa's large painted table is picked out with bold black geometric swirls against a backdrop of green, yellow and burnt umber. The accompanying set of lilac painted chairs pay homage to the Omega designs of Roger Fry, with caned backs, and rows of yellow circles on panels of powder blue. The rear of each chair is emblazoned with Virginia's initials in yellow, against a background of sage green.

Having knocked down walls to form the sitting room, Virginia created an open-plan dining area by opening up the room beside the kitchen. Into this space she introduced a set of yellow, pink and terracotta furniture from Grant and Bell's 1932 Music Room exhibition at the Lefevre Gallery. Virginia funded the launch event, and paid for a third of the costs, hosting 'a quite ghastly party … a purely commercial (don't whisper it) affair, to induce the rich to buy furniture, and so employ a swarm of poor scarecrows who are languishing in Fitzroy Street'. Cyril Connolly provided an ecstatic account of the evening – 'the room vibrated to a Debussy solo on the harp', the music blending with 'the surrounding patterns of flowers and falling leaves in a rare union of intellect and imagination, colour and sound, which produced in the listener a momentary apprehension of the life of the spirit, that lovely and un-English credo'.

Despite the enticement of 'boys in white jackets handing blue, green and yellow drinks' almost nothing sold, so Virginia came away with a set of dining chairs embroidered in pink and yellow,

and a terracotta music cabinet enlivened by black criss-cross lines. Today the cabinet sits beneath Vanessa's 1912 portrait of Virginia, a testament to sisterly generosity and patronage. Hopefully her Sussex guests would have caught a hint of the 'riotous sense of colour' and 'romantic splendour' praised by Connolly, who felt the artists had created 'a great canvas of autumn; not the usual drooling sickbed of countryside, but those conjunctions of sun and wind that suddenly illuminate gardens and beech woods'.

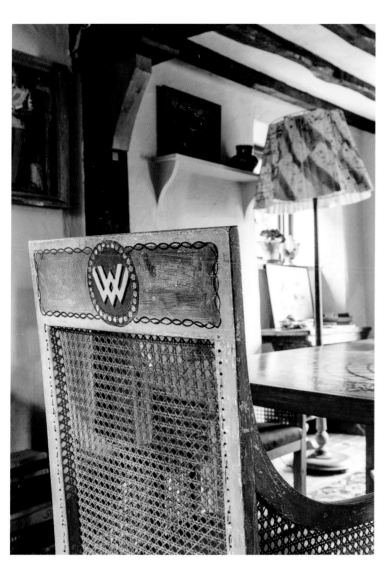

LEFT: Table and chairs commissioned by Virginia for Monk's House, Vanessa Bell, 1929–30.

ABOVE: Chairs designed by Vanessa Bell for Monk's House, emblazoned with Virginia's initials in yellow against a background of sage green.

TOP RIGHT: Table-top view of the 1929–30 Omega-style table designed by Vanessa Bell for Monk's House. Painted in bold geometric patterns on a ground of yellow, green and burnt umber.

ABOVE: *Newhaven Harbour* by Vanessa Bell, 1936 (Sitting Room).

ABOVE: View of the Dining Room, showing
the set of Grant and Bell chairs from the 1932
Music Room exhibition at the Lefevre Gallery.

LEFT: *The Forum, Rome,* by Virginia's
nephew Quentin Bell, 1935.

ABOVE: Close-up view of the 1932 Music Room chairs designed by Grant and Bell, with embroidered panels showing autumnal scenes of pink flowers against a bright yellow background, blue seascapes beyond.

FAR LEFT: Embroidered mirror frame designed by Duncan Grant as a Christmas present for Virginia in 1937, featuring yellow Canterbury bells against a black background.

LEFT: The entrance hall at Monk's House, featuring two Italian scenes painted by Vanessa Bell, 1912.

Conversation and Creature Comforts

After a visit to Monk's House, Clive Bell told Virginia Woolf, 'You have created an atmosphere different from, perhaps better than, any I know.' Virginia's rooms were shaped by her character – her love of people, of conversation, of colour and light. Contemporaries describe the almost iridescent experience of spending time in her company. Raymond Mortimer felt that she was 'the most enchanting conversationalist I've ever known. Jean Cocteau was perhaps a more brilliant talker, but he would give a performance, where hers you felt were entirely spontaneous – she was just letting her imagination rip.' Christopher Isherwood was equally entranced: 'We are at the tea table. Virginia is sparkling with gaiety, delicate malice and gossip ... listening to her, we missed appointments, forgot love affairs, stayed on and on into the small hours, when we had to be hinted, gently, but firmly, out of the house.'

Far from leading a solitary life, Virginia thrived on human contact: 'this social side is very genuine to me ... it is a piece of jewellery I inherit from my mother – a joy in laughter, something that is stimulated, not selfishly, wholly or vainly by contact with my friends. And then ideas leap up in me.' According to John Lehmann, 'both Leonard and Virginia were sociable people – too sociable I sometimes used to think for the continuity of Virginia's work – and liked to invite their friends for a week-end at Rodmell'. Guests may have complained about the lack of heating, and Virginia's daily writing routine, but many were content to be left to their own devices. Angus Davidson describes 'staying for a weekend at

Rodmell, as I did more than once, was a great pleasure. Virginia was a charming hostess, and unlike some hostesses, had the sensible habit of leaving one a good deal to oneself. She herself would probably be working and would disappear for a good part of the day into her hut at the far end of the orchard ... In the evenings, after dinner, we would sit talking, Virginia smoking a cheroot.'

Monk's House soon became a magnet for the same group of friends who visited Charleston, or (from 1926) Eddy Sackville-West at Knole. As well as weekends, the Woolfs were typically resident for Christmas, Easter, and several months in the summer. Virginia's letters reveal a punishing social round; in August 1935 she complained, 'since coming here I have poured out tea for 15 self-invited guests'. These casual callers were a continual source of frustration for Virginia's long suffering housekeepers, throwing their carefully calculated catering plans. In addition to the Charleston group, Maynard Keynes and Lydia Lopokova would drive from

TOP RIGHT: E.M. Forster, January 1940.

RIGHT: Lydia Lopokova, December 1931.

FAR RIGHT: Virginia Woolf reading in the upstairs sitting room, with the Vanessa Bell fireplace behind her, c1933.

ABOVE: Vita Sackville-West,
September 1932.

Tilton Farmhouse, and the parties would enjoy endless games of bowls on Leonard's carefully tended terrace lawn. Eddy was also a regular visitor to Monk's House, popping over for tea from Knole. After a visit in August 1928 Virginia wrote a lyrical passage in her diary, musing on the impressions left by people, substantial or insubstantial: 'Eddy has just gone, leaving me the usual feeling: why is not human intercourse more definite, tangible; why aren't I left holding a small round substance, say of the size of a pea, in my hand; something I can put in a box & look at?' Virginia felt 'there is so little left. Yet these people one sees are fabric only made once in the world; these contacts we have are unique; and if E. were, say killed tonight,

LEFT: Virginia Woolf and Dadie Rylands, September 1932.

nothing definite would happen to me; yet his substance is never again to be repeated.'

Many friends like Lytton Strachey, T.S. Eliot and E.M. Forster were persuaded to stay the night, enjoying increasing levels of comfort as the years went by. However physically warm they might be, most guests eagerly anticipated the wry humour and sexual candour of fireside conversation. Vita Sackville-West summed up a consummate Bloomsbury mingling of art and life when she wrote to her husband in June 1926: 'I am as you see [from the letterhead] staying with Virginia. She is sitting opposite, embroidering a rose, a black lace fan, a box of matches and four playing cards, on a mauve canvas background, from a design by her sister, and from time to time she says, "you have written enough, let us now talk about copulation".'

E.M. Forster enjoyed drunken evenings talking about 'sodomy and saphho with emotion', while for Elizabeth Bowen 'the main impression was of a creature of laughter and movement ... her power of conveying enjoyment was extraordinary. And her laughter was entrancing ... As it happened, the last day I saw her I was staying at Rodmell and I remember her kneeling back on the floor – we were tacking away, mending a torn Spanish curtain in the house – and she sat back on her heels and put her head back in a patch of sun, early spring sun. Then she laughed in this consuming, choking, delightful, hooting way. And that is what has remained with me.'

As Leonard knew all too well, Virginia's moods could slip suddenly from joy to abject sadness, signalling the onset of breakdown. After a dramatic incident at Quentin Bell's birthday party, Leonard remained constantly vigilant, ready to suggest that she slip away to another room if over-sensitised. It was a difficult judgement to make – as Virginia wrote to Ethel Smyth, her illness was a constant source of creativity: 'Madness is terrific ... and in its lava I still find most of the things I write about.' For some, this could be unsettling. Raymond Mortimer described the way 'her fancy got going very often on yourself, the person she was talking to. And she began imagining what your life was, and then gradually her novelist's imagination took charge, and instead of going on asking you what you did, she began to build up the most extraordinary sort of inverted pyramid of what she imagined your life was.'

ABOVE: Virginia and John Lehmann sitting beside the pond, September 1931.

ABOVE: Marjorie Strachey, James Strachey and Virginia sitting under a tree, June 1934.

ABOVE: Angelica Garnett, Clive Bell, Virginia and Maynard Keynes sitting outside the Writing Lodge, August 1935.

A Room of One's Own

1929–1930

Monk's House may have been a place of entertainment, but it was also a place of work – the home of two writers and publishers, each of whom needed space to write, and to store their ever-growing collection of books. Visitors could be rationed more easily in Sussex than in London, and if left alone, the Woolfs would retreat into a quietly productive routine: writing in the morning, walks in the afternoon, evenings spent reading or listening to music. Monk's House soon became an essential part of Virginia's creative life: 'One lives in the brain there – I slip easily from writing to reading with spaces between of walking – walking through the long grass in the meadows, or up the downs.'

Walking helped Virginia shape the flow of her sentences, and puzzled villagers would often see her mouthing words as she strode along. She would also talk to herself in the bath, her words echoing through to the cook working in the kitchen below. As Leonard explained, 'She always said the sentences out loud that she had written during the night. She needed to know if they sounded right, and the bath was a good resonant place for trying them out.' Initial ideas would be sketched out using a writing board on her lap, then taken to her writing lodge in the garden to be worked up in more detail. But the writing lodge could be cold in the winter, and Virginia dreamed of creating a room she could use in all weathers.

'A woman must have money and a room of her own if she is to write fiction.' Virginia was busy working on *A Room of One's Own* when her

dream became a reality. By spring 1929 *Orlando* was selling so well that Virginia could write triumphantly in her diary: 'After all, I say, I made £1000 all from willing it early one morning. No more poverty, I said; & poverty has ceased. I am summoning Philcox next week to plan a room – I have money to build it, money to furnish it.' With the help of architect G.L. Kennedy, Philcox Brothers duly built a plain two-storey extension for £320. Leonard dealt with the paperwork, but Virginia supervised every element of the work: 'If convenient to you, Mrs Woolf will come down and meet you at your office in Lewes on Thursday morning next in order to choose colours of paint for the two new rooms and to settle about bricks for the fireplace.'

Virginia indulged her love of green, selecting pale green distemper for the walls, and blue for the linking staircase to the first floor. The upstairs space became a cosy sitting room, used by the Woolfs after dinner, and whenever they had small numbers of guests. Nearly every photograph of Virginia at Rodmell after 1929 was taken in this room; in the background you can usually catch a glimpse of the fireplace tiles painted by Vanessa Bell, with an overflowing fruit bowl and sinuous lilies. The downstairs space became Virginia's bedroom, accessible only via a single door to the garden, with a path leading directly to the writing lodge beyond. Virginia loved the 'vast sweeping views',

RIGHT: Virginia's bedroom at Monk's House, finished in 1930.

ABOVE: The fireplace tiles designed by Vanessa Bell, showing a sailing ship with a lighthouse in the distance. Inscribed 'VW from VB 1930'.

and the sense of the garden all around 'where the rising sun on the apples & asparagus wakes me if I leave the curtain open'. In 1930 she told Ethel Smyth of her intention to: 'smell a red rose ... gently surge across the lawn ... light a cigarette, take my writing board on my knee; and let myself down, like a diver, very cautiously into the last sentence I wrote yesterday.'

Everything in this much-loved space was intensely personal to Virginia. The tiles around the fireplace are inscribed 'VW from VB 1930', and depict a sailing ship with a lighthouse beyond. This double reference links both to Virginia's 1927 book *To the Lighthouse*, for which Vanessa designed the cover, and to the Cornish lighthouse they had loved as children when holidaying in St Ives. Virginia told her sister, 'your style is unique: because so truthful; and therefore it upsets one completely'. Virginia's narrow bed lies to the right of the fireplace, and in her lifetime it rested against bookshelves filled with the *Dictionary of National Biography*, edited by her father Sir Leslie Stephen. To the left of the fireplace the matching shelves contained all the first editions of her books published around the world, in every possible language.

Today the room is filled with pictures by Vanessa Bell, Duncan Grant and their daughter Angelica Garnett. In the corner stands a delicate green bookcase, filled with volumes of Shakespeare. Each book is encased in a handmade cover of abstract design, created by Virginia during one of her periods of mental illness. Unable to write, she produced these hauntingly beautiful works of art as a distraction, each of the soft colours bleeding into the next, forming a sad but pleasing whole. Cherished despite its association with difficult times, the bookcase once stood to the right of the fireplace in Tavistock Square. It moved with the Woolfs to Mecklenburgh Square in 1939, and was finally evacuated to Monk's House when their London home was bombed in October 1940.

Woolf spent most of September and October 1940 at Monk's House, coming up to London every week or so 'to see more of Bloomsbury destroyed'. At Tavistock Square she looked up to see 'one glass door in the next door house hanging; I cd [sic] just see a piece of my studio wall standing; otherwise rubble where I wrote so many books. Open air where we sat so many nights, gave so many parties.'

Mecklenburgh Square was damaged but not completely destroyed; many precious objects were salvaged from the dust-filled rooms: 'Duncan's glasses, Nessa's plates ... How I worked to buy them – one by one.' Partly distressed, partly relieved, Virginia regretted having to wind her way through the piles of displaced furniture and books at Monk's.

Depression descended after Christmas. On 28 March 1941 Virginia spent the morning writing in her Lodge. At 11am she returned to the house, and took a half-hour rest. Having told Leonard that she would be going out for a walk, she picked up her coat and stick and set off for the water meadows. Last seen by farm-worker John Hubbard walking towards the River Ouse, she placed a heavy stone in her pocket and entered the water. Her body was finally found, floating near Asheham, three weeks later.

LEFT: The green bookcase from Tavistock Square, containing Virginia's handmade book covers.

ABOVE: On the mantel sits a favourite still life by Vanessa Bell, along with a
purple and gold cup from the Foley tea service designed by Vanessa Bell.

ABOVE: *Dead Game* by Virginia's niece Angelica Garnett, *c*1939–40.

ABOVE: *Vase and Vegetables* by Vanessa Bell, 1928–30.

RIGHT: *Monk's House* by Duncan Grant, 1930–35.

FAR RIGHT: *Monk's House Garden* by Duncan Grant, 1923.

Vita's Writing Room in the Tower at Sissinghurst.

VITA SACKVILLE WEST

Vita Sackville-West, Sissinghurst, 1930

On 16 October 1930, Vita Sackville-West spent her first night at Sissinghurst, sleeping in the tall tower of pale pink brick which rises above the remnants of a great Elizabethan house. Here at last was a building worthy of the ornate cargo of possessions she had carried from home to home. Here was a tower to rival her cousin Eddy's at Knole. Here was a ruin she could rescue and make her own.

Looking back in later years, she remembered how it 'caught instantly at my heart and my imagination. I saw what might be made of it. It was Sleeping Beauty's castle.' Her poem *Sissinghurst*, written in 1930 and dedicated to Virginia Woolf, records her sense of thankful surrender:

> A tired swimmer in the waves of time
> I throw my hands up: let the surface close:
> Sink down through centuries to another clime
> And buried find the castle and the rose

From these romantic ruins Vita and her husband Harold fashioned a patchwork home which suited their complicated patchwork household. Looking back in 1940, Vita noted 'it could not be claimed, even by a house agent, that Sissinghurst was a very convenient residence. Living in four separate bits of a building, a considerable distance apart, it may be delightful to cross moonlit quadrangles on a warm summer evening on one's way to bed, but on snowy nights it is less agreeable. It is the penalty one has to pay for living in a house which, whatever else it may be, is not orthodox.'

Happily embracing the unorthodox in her domestic arrangements, Vita liked to quote these lines from *The Prophet* by Kahlil Gibran:

> But let there be spaces in your togetherness ...
> Love one another, but make not a bond of love ...
> Fill each other's cup but drink not from one cup.

Separate living helped Vita and Harold sustain a happy marriage alongside many same-sex relationships. As well as their two sons, Sissinghurst needed to accommodate different partners at different times. Harold worked in London during the week, sharing his life with a series of younger men. Vita's lovers stayed while Harold was away, tactfully returning to London on Saturday mornings. Sometimes there were overlaps. Visiting in 1932, James Lees-Milne remembered seeing the two boys swimming in the lake: 'As we approached we heard one say – no doubt he thought *sotto voce* – to the other, breast stroking beside him, "Who is that little pansy in the yellow pullover?" "Oh", said the other disdainfully, "presumably one of Daddy's new friends."'

RIGHT: Vita Sackville-West, photographed by Lenare, and inscribed 'Eddy from Vita'.

This carefully choreographed pattern
of living was adapted in 1933 to include
Harold's sister Gwen. Sent to the countryside
to recover after a car accident, Gwen suffered
a personal and religious crisis. Vita created a
bedroom for Gwen in the Tower, nursed her
through endless operations, and took her on
long holidays abroad. The sisters-in-law fell
in love, and Gwen remained at Sissinghurst
until 1940. Her constant presence gives new
meaning to Nigel Nicolson's description of
'living in a village-house, where different
members of the family could live apart from
each other and meet communally for meals'.
The multi-layered spaces that Vita and Harold
shaped at Sissinghurst are full of associative
memory, each object combining to form a
portrait of a highly unusual marriage.

RIGHT: Vita and Harold in the Writing Room
at Sissinghurst, 1930.

FAR RIGHT: The Tower at Sissinghurst; the
Writing Room is on the first floor, and Gwen's
bedroom was at the top.

Sissinghurst, showing South Cottage on the left,
with the Tower and South Wing beyond.

Lost Edwardian Worlds

One of the things that drew Vita and Harold together was their shared experience of opulent childhoods. Both had grown up in extraordinary surroundings, enjoying levels of beauty and luxury they could never hope to replicate in their adult lives. The income from Vita's family trust was generous, but it would not provide her with a home on the scale of Knole. For Vita, the great house would always be a difficult memory, a 'torture treat', captivatingly described in *Orlando*, but painful to visit after the death of her father in 1928. In *The Edwardians*, published in 1930, Vita expressed her own sense of love and loss for the Sackville heirlooms left behind in the echoing chambers of her youth:

> *The old rooms, in the candlelight, inspired him with a tenderness*
> *he would not by daylight have credited. Their beauty, which*
> *he had thought to be exterior, became significant; they were*
> *quickened by the breath of some existence which they had once*
> *enjoyed, when no eye regarded them as a museum, but took them*
> *for granted as the natural setting for daily life; and that applied*
> *to their furnishings too, to the mirrors into whose dim pools*
> *women had stolen many a frank or furtive glance; to the chairs*
> *whose now faded velvets had received the weight of limbs*
> *regardless of mud on the boots.*

Dismissed by the Sackvilles as a 'penniless third secretary', Harold was dependent on the income he earned, firstly from the Foreign Office, and later as a writer and politician. The younger son of a successful diplomat, his childhood holidays were spent in the majestic Irish houses of his wealthy maternal relations: austere turreted Killyleagh, classical Clandeboye, and the fantastical toy fort of Shanganagh. When not in Ireland, he and his siblings followed their parents from embassy to embassy: 'My father during all the years of my childhood and boyhood lived abroad. The pantechnicon vans would roll across the Caspian, the Mediterranean or the Aegean, and there, in a house which looked now on the Adrassy Strasse, now upon the Golden Horn, now towards Trafalgar, or now across the Neva to the fortress of St Peter and St Paul, the Nicolson home would be reconstructed.' According to Norman Rose, Harold judged each residence by the grandeur of their dining rooms. In Istanbul the 'soft Bosphorus sunset slid across the white dinner table in slatted shafts of orange and blue'; in Tangier the table was weighed down with exotic flowers and silver bowls of sugared almonds; in Madrid the scarlet damask walls and royal portraits failed to distract from the strong smell of the stables opposite.

Thanks to her mother, Vita's frame of reference was equally international. Lady Sackville, known as 'Bonne Maman', was the illegitimate daughter of Spanish dancer Pepita and Lionel, 2nd Baron Sackville. She had been brought up in France, always speaking with a lilting French accent. From her admirer Sir John Murray Scott, Lady Sackville inherited a vast apartment on the Rue Lafitte in Paris, filled with precious pieces from Lord Hertford's collection at the Chateau de Bagatelle. As a little girl, Vita would stand, bored 'while visitors

RIGHT: Knole, Vita's childhood home.

LEFT: The King's Room, Knole.

RIGHT: Killyleagh Castle, the
Northern Irish seat of Harold
Nicolson's grandparents.

marvelled at the furniture ... Louis quatorze, Louis quinze, Louis seize, Directoire, Empire – all those were names, half meaningless, which I absorbed till they became as familiar as bread, milk, water, butter.'

Blessed with eclectic tastes and an obsessive collecting habit, Lady Sackville kept up with every artistic fashion: she was sculpted by Auguste Rodin, used Edwin Lutyens to remodel her houses, and took Vita to see Augustus John in his studio. Her decorating shop, Speall's, was one of the first to promote the style of Sergei Diaghilev's *Ballet Russe*. She used her Brighton house to experiment with designs, and in 1918 Vita was the lucky recipient of a room inspired by Russian painter and theatre designer Léon Bakst. Lady Sackville's diary records the vibrant outcome: 'Her walls are of shiny emerald green paper, floor green; doors and furniture sapphire blue; ceiling apricot colour. Curtains blue and inside curtains yellowish. The decoration of the furniture is mainly beads of all colours painted on the blue ground; even the door plates are treated the same. I have 6 bright orange pots on her green marble mantelpiece, and there are salmon and tomato-colour cushions and lampshades. Pictures by Bakst, George Plank, Rodin, and framed in passe-partout ribbons'.

RIGHT: Vita's mother, Lady Sackville, sculpted by Auguste Rodin, 1913.

LEFT: Image of a Baccante from *The Decorative Art of Léon Bakst*, 1913. Vita's mother was an early promoter of Sergei Diaghilev's *Ballet Russe*, and gave a copy of this book to her daughter.

'What the tide rolls to her feet'

Virginia Woolf was surprisingly critical of Vita's own decorative approach: 'she never breaks fresh ground. She picks up what the tide rolls to her feet. For example, she follows, with simple instinct, all the inherited tradition of furnishing, so that her house is gracious, glowing, stately, but without novelty or adventure.' Piqued by Vita's rejection of Bloomsbury aesthetics – all products of the Omega Workshops were condemned as 'horrible' – Virginia ignored the eclectic influence of Lady Sackville, and the legacy of Knole and Rue Lafitte. Having been exposed to works of art of the finest calibre from an early age, Vita found it difficult to admire the British post-impressionists. Virginia ruefully remembered Vita causing great offence to Roger Fry with her habit of 'praising & talking indiscriminately about art, which goes down in her set, but not in ours'.

Vita may not have embraced Bloomsbury design, but she did inherit her mother's love for dramatic colour combinations and theatrical groupings of unusual objects. Mercurial in temperament, Lady Sackville was prone to acts of random generosity, filling each of Vita's homes with eccentric gifts: Japanese gardens made of stone flowers; carved life-size fruit and vegetables; purple Persian glass; tables topped with lapis lazuli. Some of these pieces had been cobbled together via her decorating shop, Speall's; others were remnants of the Hertford collection salvaged from Rue Lafitte. Chief amongst these were a set of bronze garden urns from the Chateau de Bagatelle, and the 62 'oil paintings on copper, representing Eastern figures' which wind their way up the staircase to Vita's writing room at Sissinghurst.

ABOVE: Gifts from Lady Sackville: jewelled Japanese garden, Writing Room.

RIGHT: Gifts from Lady Sackville: carved fruit and vegetables, Long Library.

With the Nicolson finances perpetually in flux, Harold was happy
to receive Lady Sackville's bounty, however heavy the emotional toll
extracted in return. Delighting in a set of Persian carpets 'moth-
eaten but superb', Harold wrote in his 1932 diary: 'It is typical of
our existence that with no settled income and no certain prospects
we should live in a muddle of museum carpets, ruined castles, and
penury. Yet we know very well that all this uncertainty is better for
us than a dull and unadventurous security.' Harold had been equally
pleased with the vast collection of elaborate wedding presents the
couple were given in 1913. Displayed in the Great Hall at Knole,
and recorded in multiple press photographs, the 600 gifts included
furniture, paintings, tapestries and mirrors, as well as silver,
jewellery and objets d'art.

As a daughter, Vita was not entitled to remove any heirlooms from
Knole. Her family and friends responded by giving the young couple
objects which looked as if they could have belonged to the Sackvilles
for centuries. Some of these were genuine – inlaid cabinets, carved
oak chairs – others were Edwardian replicas: ebony mirrors with
silver mounts, sconces copied from originals at Knole. All were
solemnly transported by land and sea to the Nicolsons' first home in
Istanbul, where Harold was third secretary to the British legation.
'Our house', wrote Vita, 'is the most attractive house you have ever
seen. It is a wooden Turkish house, with a little garden and a pergola
of grapes and a pomegranate tree covered with scarlet fruit, and such
a view over the Golden Horn and the sea and Santa Sophia! And on
the side of a hill, a perfect suntrap!'

Vita's photograph album shows the heavy British furniture looking
a little uneasy in the airy rooms overlooking the Bosphorus,
particularly when paired with Turkish water fountains. Everything
was duly transported back after Vita returned home for the birth
of their son Ben, finding more comfortable settings in the houses
acquired for the Nicolsons in England: 182 Ebury Street, London

ABOVE: Gifts from Lady Sackville: Persian glass,
Tower Staircase.

RIGHT: One of Vita's favourite decorative features:
coloured glass arranged against the light. This example
is from the Tower Staircase.

and Long Barn, Kent. Long Barn was bought with money from Vita's trust; Ebury Street was a gift from Lady Sackville, and remodelled at her expense by Lutyens. Press reactions were complimentary: 'The Hon Mrs Nicolson's Town House contains much to arouse the envy of artistic London, set with rare taste against a fine background of original Georgian panelling.'

Vita's London entrance hall earned particular praise, noting the careful placement of coloured glass: 'This spacious room has beautiful and ancient Eastern rugs on the marble floor, and a lovely piece of fragile 17th-century tapestry hangs on one of the walls. The room is full of colour. Charming pieces of bright blue glass placed on rose-red silk stand near the window; an amber-yellow "witches globe" shimmers near the door, while on the centre table a bouquet of golden flowers give a charming effect of subdued richness.' Faced with these stately interiors, Harold harboured the occasional desire to rebel, smuggling in modernist paintings by John Banting, and contemporary sculpture by Toma Rosandić. But on the whole he found it impossible to resist the coherence of Vita's vision: 'I do not want to make any room ugly, but I should like to feel that there were open to me, in some personal habitation, an orgy of bad taste. The bore about it is that I love Viti's taste – and never wish in reality to depart from it.'

ABOVE: Gifts from Lady Sackville: Paintings of Turkish men and women in the costumes of the court of the Ottoman Empire, by Jean Baptist Vanmour. Formerly in the Hertford Collection at the Chateau de Bagatelle.

LEFT: Vita and Harold's 600 wedding gifts, displayed in the Great Hall at Knole, 1913.

The colour scheme of the dining-room is delightfully cool and restful. The black and white marble floor is partly carpeted in black, and the pale grey walls make an admirable foil to a fine piece of 17th-century Flemish tapestry, also to some silver sconces, the originals of which are at Knole Park. Cool green curtains frame the window, which looks out on a paved garden in which fig-trees and almond-trees cast a welcome shade in summer time

...y Street with its quiet unobtrusive conceals some fine interiors and charm[ing] gardens behind its sedate frontages. No. 182 The Hon. Mr. and Mrs. Harold [Ni]cholson have made their town home. The [hou]se has preserved its original Georgian [pa]nelling intact and is pervaded by a delight[ful] atmosphere of old-fashioned charm. It [has] some interesting pictures of the French [and] Italian schools, some of which hang in [the] entrance hall, which is finely proportioned [and] simply furnished with rare pieces of old furniture

THE HON. MRS. NICHOLSON'S TOWN HOUSE CONTAINS MUCH TO AROUSE THE ENVY OF ARTISTIC LONDON, SET WITH RARE TASTE AGAINST A FINE BACKGROUND OF ORIGINAL GEORGIAN PANELLING

This spacious room has beautiful and ancient Eastern rugs on the marble floor, and a lovely piece of fragile 17th-century tapestry hangs on one of the walls. The room is full of colour. Charming pieces of bright blue glass placed on rose-red silk stand near the window, an amber-yellow "witch's globe" shimmers near the door, while on the centre table a bouquet of golden flowers give a charming effect of subdued richness

ABOVE: A further gift from Lady Sackville: Vita and Harold's first London home in Ebury Street, remodelled for them by Lutyens.

ABOVE: Interiors of Vita and Harold's house in Istanbul, 1913.

ABOVE: The 'Big Room' at Long Barn, Vita and Harold's first home in Kent.

1920–1930: 'Marriage with liaisons'

Vita and Harold's open marriage has been explored in countless books, examining the impact on their families, their writing, and the gardens they created at Long Barn and Sissinghurst. Less attention has been paid to the way their sexuality shaped the homes they shared, and the complex choreography of their queer domesticity. Shaken by the trauma of Vita's elopement with Violet Trefusis, their pattern of living in the 1920s was carefully adapted to allow the inclusion of other sexual partners. Vita summed up the arrangement in a letter of 1926, describing how 'the two people who are to achieve this odd spirito-mystico-practical unity must start with very special temperaments, i.e. it is all very well to say the ideal is "marriage with liaisons". But if you were in love with another woman, or I with another man, we should both or either of us be finding a natural sexual fulfilment which would inevitably rob our own relationship of something. As it is, the liaisons which you and I contract are something perfectly apart from the more natural attitude we have towards each other, and don't interfere.'

While Harold remained in the diplomatic service in the 1920s, separate living was simple. After the birth of their sons, Ben and Nigel, Vita remained in England, leaving Harold to his own devices in a series of flats in Paris, Tehran and Berlin. Sexual encounters were easily arranged, and only two of his many lovers impinged on life with Vita: the artist Jean de Gaigneron, who stayed at Long Barn to paint a portrait of Ben, and the writer Raymond Mortimer, who became a lifelong friend. In Paris, Harold's letters to Vita refer tactfully to evenings with 'my funny friend with a charming flat at the Rond Point', or 'my nice friend who knows all the clevers'. In Tehran, Harold entertained Raymond Mortimer for a three-month visit – 'Dearest Tray, you are so much to me ... Anyway you know that there is someone in the world to whom you are of supreme importance'. In Berlin Harold introduced Vita's cousin Eddy to the joys of gay nightlife, playing host at 24 Brucken Allee to countless friends seeking excitement in clubs like the Silhouette, the Eldorado, the Rhezi and the Salome. His diaries are peppered with references to young men like handsome Etonian Sandy Baird, 'an absolute little bum boy', and American artist Bobby Sharpe, 'very conjugal and bliss'.

Vita meanwhile was free to pursue relationships at home – all women, with the single exception of writer Geoffrey Scott. Lovers were entertained at Ebury Street and Long Barn, many leaving lyrical descriptions of their experiences. 1927 was a particularly intense period, recorded in letters to and from Virginia Woolf: 'you only be a careful dolphin in your gambolling, or you'll find Virginia's soft crevices lined with hooks'. In quick succession Vita slept with Clive Bell's mistress, Mary Hutchinson, the bisexual actress Valerie Taylor, and Mary Campbell, wife of a South African poet. Mary Hutchinson was seduced at Ebury Street, writing to retrieve her belongings: 'I left a pearl earring on the table by your bed. I remember exactly

LEFT: Vita with (from right) Ben, Nigel, and Harold's lover Raymond Mortimer, Sherfield, 1927.

where I put it, at the corner near you. Will you be very nice and post it to me soon? ... Did you sleep among the thorns and petals?' Earrings came up again with Mary Campbell, who moved with her husband into the cottage at Long Barn. Mary came home one day with cuts and bruises on her thighs, at the sight of which Roy is said to have exclaimed, 'Good heavens kid! I don't mind you sleeping with Vita, but at least get her to take her earrings off!'

Each of these escapades was happily discussed in letters to Harold; for Valerie Taylor there was an interesting overlap with Harold's former lover Raymond Mortimer, as they briefly contemplated a 'Nicolson model' marriage. As Vita told Harold: 'She let him sleep with her, but I haven't told him that she wanted to sleep with me the next night – at Oxford – I *didn't*, but that was no fault of hers. On the whole, I have encouraged a collage rather than matrimony.' Valerie stayed up late with Vita in Ebury Street, having spent the afternoon dressed as Byron – 'we talked about H writing a play about Byron in which she would act'. Small wonder that Lady Sackville was fearful of bad publicity when *Orlando* was published in 1928; she told the editor of *The Observer*, 'I have spent years, *hiding* what Harold and Vita really are', and drummed up support from Harold's worried sister: 'Gwen fears Harold will be dismissed from the service for allowing that book to be published.'

Well aware of the repercussions for Radclyffe Hall after the 1928 obscenity trial, Vita remained surprisingly insouciant about exposure. Far from hiding her relationships, Vita liked to surround herself with mementos of her former partners, many of whom worked with her to arrange or embellish her rooms. This pattern had been established early in Vita's life, when her first expression of independent taste marked her emerging sexual identity. In 1910 Vita spent a romantic spring in Italy with school friend Rosamund Grosvenor. Seduced both by Rosamund and the 'strong, luxuriant,

ABOVE: Portrait of Ben Nicolson at Long Barn by Harold's lover Jean de Gaigneron.

cruel Italy of the Renaissance', Vita asked for her room at Knole to be transformed, making it 'stern and austere, not the bedroom of a young girl'.

In 1911 she and Rosamund covered the room with renaissance-style wall paintings, featuring heraldic symbols and 'vaguely architectural towers' against a backdrop of blue and gold diaper work. Even though Vita was later to claim that her relationship with Rosamund was 'entirely physical, as to be frank, she always bored me as a companion', she treasured the intricate objects acquired for 'my Ghirlandaio Room' for the rest of her life. Kept intact until the death of her father in 1928, Vita slept in the bedroom whenever she visited Knole, sometimes using it to seduce new conquests. Both the

Italianate bed and the carved 'boy bishop's head' once housed in the shrine beside the fireplace were to end their days at Sissinghurst, giving some credence to Rosamund's suggestion that 'Men may come, and men may go, but I go on for ever.'

ABOVE: Entertaining at Long Barn: Vita's lovers Valerie Taylor and Hilda Mattheson (far left, second from left), and Harold's lover Raymond Mortimer (third from right).

FAR LEFT: 'My Ghirlandaio Room' – Vita's Renaissance bedroom at Knole, painted with mock-Italian frescoes in 1911 by Vita and her lover Rosamund Grosvenor.

LEFT: The 18th-century torchère from Vita's bedroom at Knole, now in the Long Library at Sissinghurst.

RIGHT: The 'boy bishop's head' from Vita's room at Knole, proudly displayed in her bedroom at Sissinghurst.

New Beginnings: King's Bench Walk

January 1930

1930 signalled a change in the Nicolson marital dynamic: Harold resigned from the Foreign Office, and returned to England to take up the role of London Diarist at the *Evening Standard*. Swift adjustments were required now that both members of the partnership were suddenly in the same country. As Vita wrote to Virginia: 'it is always complicated when he comes home ... all sorts of different landscapes seem to open whichever way I look'. Ebury Street had been sold, so a new London base was required for Harold's use during the week. His brother, Freddy, came to the rescue: as a barrister, he was entitled to use first floor chambers in the Temple at 4, King's Bench Walk. No longer needing them, he allowed Harold to register under his name.

Sought out as homes for bachelors, rooms in this appealing row of late 17th-century houses had the masculine feel of an Oxford college. Behind the soft red brick exteriors lay attractively panelled interiors; each set had a spacious sitting room, two bedrooms and a tiny kitchen. Having a degree from Oxford even entitled Harold to become a member of the Temple; on payment of a small fee he gained the right to 'eat in the hall, use the library, have food sent in from the kitchen and pray in the chapel'. Here was the perfect setting for a gay life as independent as the one previously enjoyed in Berlin; Vita seldom intruded, preferring to stay with friends on her increasingly rare visits to London.

Consulting Harold by letter, Vita readied the flat for his arrival. James Lees-Milne provided a detailed description of her decorative approach. The panelling was painted in old ivory; a faded Persian carpet found for the floor, a Queen Anne walnut bureau placed between the windows, a long oak table against the wall, with straight backed cane-seated side chairs and comfortable armchairs. She filled the shelves with books, and covered the walls with Harold's favourite paintings. In generous concession to his modernist tastes, she bought a beautiful Duncan Grant for his birthday. This was duly hung over the fireplace, described by Vita as 'the port of Marseille (with a big sailing ship in it) and a peach-coloured tower that goes wriggling down in reflections in the water. It is the most romantic thing you ever saw, and a lovely colour.'

From 1932 onwards, Harold shared Kings Bench Walk with a series of young lodgers, many of whom were friends of his sons Ben and Nigel. According to the author Michael Bloch, 'Harold had a strong libido and sought a daily erotic adventure well into middle age ... he created a circle of attractive, well-bred young men of literary bent, who in return for his hospitality and mentorship were happy to oblige him with his somewhat unromantic urges.' Christopher Hobhouse was the first to move in, followed in 1934 by James Lees-Milne. Both were friends of the irrepressible James Pope-Hennessy; handsome and troubled, James toyed with both Nigel and Harold's affections. A set of photographs from autumn 1936 show James and Christopher at Sissinghurst, with Nigel sitting somewhat uneasily between.

RIGHT: King's Bench Walk in the Temple, London.

ABOVE: Harold's cosy sitting room at King's Bench Walk.

RIGHT: Nigel Nicolson at Sissinghurst with two friends who became lovers of his father: Christopher Hobhouse (foreground), Harold's first lodger at King's Bench Walk, and James Pope-Hennessy (right).

FAR RIGHT: A John Banting painting from Harold's personal collection, showing two naked men divided by a screen.

Sissinghurst

April 1930

With Harold safely ensconced in King's Bench Walk – 'too lovely for words' – Vita could begin to think about more ambitious projects. Although full of rustic charm and historic associations (rumoured to be the birthplace of Caxton), Long Barn lacked architectural distinction. It could never hope to take the place of Knole in Vita's heart, a feeling which had grown since her father's death in 1928. As she wrote to her son Ben – 'it has to do with Grandpapa's death, and the three or four days in which I had to rule Knole and make every decision ... But I had to do it, and it really marked a turning point in my life. In fact my mental muscles grew surprisingly, and I have never been quite the same since.' With her cousin Eddy in the Gatehouse Tower, and his father stripping treasures from the state rooms to pay death duties, Vita felt increasingly alienated from her childhood home.

Harold's lover, James Lees-Milne, who knew them both, observed the 'strange emotional duet' that played out between Vita and Eddy: 'Vita resented the fact that she had been born a girl, whereas Eddy may have regretted being born a boy. Vita loved Knole with such an atavistic passion that it was a torture of the psyche that she would never own it. Eddy who was not brought up there as a child was bored by Knole and dreaded the responsibility of ownership and burden.' Over the course of 1929 Eddy took on the role of go-between, driving over to Long Barn to break the news of sales. One of the most deeply regretted was the tapestry from the Chapel, where Vita and Harold had been married: 'I don't know what they got for it; I wouldn't ask. It was announced on the wireless, in the News, funny ...

ABOVE and RIGHT: Sissinghurst – for Vita an 'ancestral mansion', and a suitable replacement for Knole.

Anyway, I am never going to Knole again; or perhaps just once before I die.'

On 4 March 1930, Westwood, the adjoining farm to Long Barn, was bought by poultry farmers. Horrified by the prospect of chicken houses suddenly appearing all around her, Vita was prompted to action. Lunching in Sussex with her former lover Dorothy Wellesley,

she asked Dorothy's land agent Donald Beale for advice. He mentioned that an unusual property with Sackville connections was on the market, only 20 miles east of Long Barn. On 4 April 1930, Donald drove Dorothy and Vita and her younger son Nigel over to Sissinghurst. Vita fell 'flat in love'. That evening Harold wrote in his diary, 'Vita telephones to say she has seen the ideal house – a place in Kent near Cranbrook.' The next day, he and their elder son Ben jumped on the train to Staplehurst, and described rounding the corner to see 'a view of the two towers as we approach. We go round carefully in the mud. I am cold and calm but I like it.'

Sissinghurst had a double family connection: Sir John Baker, Chancellor of the Exchequer to Henry VIII, had bought the site in 1533. Not only did he marry a Sackville – Catherine – but their daughter Cecily Baker was to marry Vita's direct ancestor, Sir Thomas Sackville, 1st Earl of Dorset. It boasted a fine brick entrance gateway built in the 1530s, with porters' lodges to either side, exactly as at Knole. Beyond the gateway Catherine Sackville's son, Sir Richard Baker, had built an extraordinary Renaissance-style courtyard house, ready for the visit of Queen Elizabeth in 1573.

The Bakers suffered during the Civil War; their estate was divided between daughters, and the house was abandoned, gradually falling into decline. During the 18th century it was further damaged when used to house French prisoners from

RIGHT: Eddy Sackville-West at Sissinghurst with the Nicolsons, 1932.

the Seven Years War. All that survived by 1930 was the dramatic central tower, with its two side turrets, and two small remnants: a banqueting house to the north, called the Priest's House, and a small portion of one of the courtyards, known as the South Cottage.

The Sissinghurst estate also featured an eminently practical Victorian gothic 'Castle Residence', built in the 1850s for the gentleman tenant of the accompanying 478-acre farm. Most buyers would have wanted to use the seven bedrooms, four staff bedrooms, lawns, shrubberies, gardens, greenhouse and vinery. For Vita this held no romance; her preference was for 'the remains of Sissinghurst Castle close by, which are a prominent and pleasing feature in the property and full of historic interest'. With the support of Lady Sackville, she persuaded her family trustees to raise a loan of £12,000 to buy the estate. Harold was all too aware of the amount of money it would take to make the changes needed, but he realised that it held an irresistible allure for his wife: 'Through its veins pulses the blood of the Sackville dynasty. True that it comes through the female line – but then we are both feminist and after all Knole came in the same way. It is for you an ancestral mansion.'

LEFT: From Vita's collection at Sissnghurst: photograph of her cousin, inscribed 'Eddy for Vita, Christmas 1934'.

The Tower 1930–1933
'In the high room where tall the shadows tilt'

Vita's first step was to take possession of the commanding space on the first floor of the great tower – 'the high room where tall the shadows tilt'. Eddy's Music Room may have marked the threshold to Knole, but Vita's Writing Room was to become the beating heart of Sissinghurst. Like Eddy, she decorated the space with the help of her lovers, each object replete with associative memory. Like Eddy, she surrounded herself with familiar books and favourite images, writing at an oak desk lit from a high latticed window. While Eddy's world looked forward to the bright colours of Bloomsbury and the Jazz Age, Vita's world looked backward, to the verdure greens and tobacco browns of fading 17th-century tapestry. Counterpoints were provided by her trademark coloured glass – placed against the light in window embrasures – and by vivid blue pottery from Harold's posting in Tehran. Local builders H.C. Punnett erected simple oak shelves and a plain corner fireplace, creating an octagonal library in the side turret. Some of the touches were intensely personal: Vita painted the cabinet above her desk a deep bronze green, and designed the capacious daybed, upholstered in dark olive elephant cord.

Driving over from Long Barn, Vita was in the happy position of getting one house ready while still occupying another. In the early days her two main handmaidens were Virginia Woolf, who introduced her to a helpful antique dealer in Warren Street, and Hilda Matheson, her lover from 1928–31. Each played their part in 'firsts' for Sissinghurst. From Virginia's friend Hugo, Vita bought an oak table, a Spanish walnut table, an oak cupboard and two chairs. Vita and Harold were there to receive the delivery – 'we carried it up, and had our tea at a table, for the first time in our history at Sissinghurst'. In October 1930, Hilda was the first person to spend the night at Sissinghurst with Vita; Harold arrived the next evening – 'we sleep at the top of the tower on two camp beds. We read by candles'. Hilda, who was Director of Talks for the BBC, helped the Nicolsons in many ways. She arranged for lucrative speaking engagements on the radio, and heaved furniture about whenever required. A typical diary entry from 1930 reads: 'Hilda and I spent the whole day at Sissinghurst arranging Harold's sitting room, bedroom and my bedroom. Paige came over from Long Barn with a lorry of furniture.'

With the bones of the Writing Room in place, Vita could begin to add the layers described by her grandson Adam Nicolson as 'an assembled world ... a form of self-portrait'. Books form the core – 2,700 arranged in subject order, the working library of a prolific author and poet. There are collections of books on gardening, travel and the lives of saints – all reflecting subjects Vita researched for her writing. There are over 450 books of poetry: seven volumes each of William Yeats and Stephen Spender, ten of T. S. Eliot, fifteen of Edith Sitwell, with Cecil Day-Lewis, Edmund Blunden, Roy Campbell, Walter de la Mare and Robert Bridges generously represented. Twenty-four books by Virginia Woolf are grouped together, including the dedication copy of *Orlando* which Vita had read for the first time on 11 October 1928 – 'a book unique in English literature ... I feel infinitely honoured at having been the peg on which it was hung and very humble.'

LEFT: Vita's Writing Room in the Tower.

ABOVE: Vita's Writing Room – Vita designed the daybed (left), and painted the corner cupboard (right) bronze green.

Equally intriguing is the large section on sex and psychology, with works by Havelock Ellis, Otto Weininger, Gerald Heard and Ernest Jones. Vita's copy of Edward Carpenter's *The Intermediate Sex* is annotated 'Middlesex' on the cover – a comment which would have appealed to Vita's new love of 1931, journalist Evelyn Irons. This relationship overlapped with the building work at Sissinghurst: on 4 March Vita invited her to lunch at King's Bench Walk; two days later Evelyn was in Kent, sitting 'in front of the fire in your room at Sissinghurst, looking at you and thinking that I had fallen in love with you, not dreaming that you would ever be in love with me,

and yet feeling tremendously happy and excited'. After that, Evelyn was up and down to Kent, helping Vita with the garden. It was during these months that Vita began to habitually adopt the uniform of whipcord breeches and high boots with laced canvas uppers that she had first experimented with at Long Barn. Evelyn felt they both had 'hermaphrodite minds', noting that 'such is our inter-homosexual homosexuality that we do not take advantage of this arrangement, but choose to appear in similar roles. On Friday, for instance, it will be gardener and water boy.'

LEFT: The shelves behind the daybed hold 24 books by Virginia Woolf.

FAR LEFT: Vita's desk, with photographs of Harold and Virginia.

Vita's Writing Room is filled with the memories of other lovers. Vita had first walked the streets dressed as 'Julian' when she eloped with Violet Trefusis, and Violet's drawing of Vita in male clothing is preserved at Sissinghurst. On the mantelshelf Vita placed the Chinese crystal rabbits given to her by Violet; on her writing desk the red lava ring presented by Violet in 1908 as the first token of her love, displayed on a lapis lazuli stand; under the shelves in her library the Gladstone bag containing the handwritten 'confession' of their affair. On the walls she hung the picture of Long Barn painted by Mary Campbell in 1927, during the months when Vita inspired such violent jealousy in her husband Roy that he attacked Mary with a knife. Vita also preserved some of the frantic messages Mary wrote on torn pieces of paper: 'Is the night never coming again when I can spend hours in your arms, when I can realise your big sort of protectiveness all round me, and be quite naked except for a covering of your rose-leaf kisses?'

Virginia Woolf appears in many places: on the writing desk, in a formal photograph taken by Lenare in 1929; pinned to the end of a bookcase, looking thoughtful in a framed holiday snap taken by Vita. This records their trip to Burgundy in the autumn of 1928 – returning one week before the publication of *Orlando*. This was the only time they went away together, and held a special significance for both of them. Five years later Vita wrote to Virginia asking if she remembered the night 'when I came along the dark passage to your room in a thunderstorm and we lay talking about whether we were frightened to death or not? That is the sort of occasion on which the things I want to say to you – and to you only – get said.' It was on this holiday that Virginia confided her dislike of 'the possessiveness and love of domination in men. In fact she dislikes the quality of masculinity. Says women stimulate her imagination, by their grace and their art of life.'

ABOVE: Vita's Writing Room – close up of windowsill.

RIGHT: Amongst the blue glass and ceramics on the chimneypiece sit two crystal rabbits given to Vita by Violet Trefusis.

Images of two other important figures were cleared from Vita's desk in the days following her death, and are preserved in a briefcase stored in the Writing Room. The first is a profile shot, in a tiny silver frame, of Christopher St John (born Christabel Marshall), who fell in love with Vita in 1932. Dismissed by a jealous Virginia as 'that mule-faced harridan of yours', Chris St John occupied a special place in Vita's heart. She bequeathed Vita an intensely felt love journal and several of her most precious possessions. A suffragette, playwright, journalist and biographer, she was also an expert calligrapher.

Two examples of her work were chosen by Vita for the Writing Room. One, always propped on the desk, quotes Phineas Fletcher, the 16th-century clergyman poet of Cranbrook, whose poem *Laetemur in Ea* opens with the following lines: 'Ah! might I in some humble Kentish dale for ever spend my slow paced hours'. Chris presented this to Vita on 10 August 1933, the first anniversary of their meeting, decorated with their initials in gold, interlaced. The second, hung on the wall, was Chris's gift to Vita in December 1933, recording her unswerving loyalty:

ABOVE: Vita's holiday snap of Virginia, taken on their trip to Burgundy in 1928.

LEFT: A formal photograph of Virginia Woolf taken in 1929 by Lenare – displayed by Vita on her writing desk.

To the love of his constant heart

As I have been
So will I ever be
Unto my death and longer if
I might.
have I of love the friendly looking eye
have I of fortune favour or despite,
I am of rock by proof as you
may see,
Not made of wax nor of no metal light
As leef to die, by change as to deceive,
Or break the promise made. And so I leave.

Tottel's Miscellany, 1557

ABOVE: Vita's sex and psychology bookshelf.

LEFT: A group of blue Persian ceramics from Vita's journey to Tehran in 1926. Vita presented one of this set to Virginia.

RIGHT: Vita's Library in the Corner Turret, immediately next to her Writing Room.

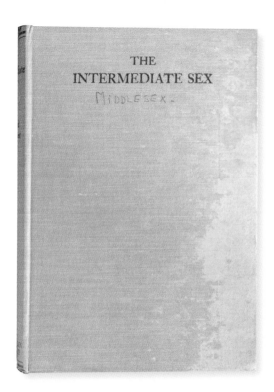

ABOVE: Vita's copy of *The Intermediate Sex*, annotated in her own hand with 'Middlesex'.

RIGHT: Vita's lover Mary Campbell, who moved with her husband into the cottage at Long Barn, 1927–28.

LEFT: Chinese crystal rabbits given to Vita by Violet Trefusis.

FAR LEFT: Vita's lover Violet Trefusis, by Sir John Lavery.

ABOVE: Painting of Long Barn by Mary Campbell, 1927.

OC DIES X AVGVSTI MCMXXXII OC

LAETEMVR IN EA

Ah! might I in some humble Kentish dale
For ever eas'ly spend my slow-paced hours.
Much should I scorn fair Eton's pleasant vale,
Or Windsor, Tempe's self, and proudest towers:
There would I sit safe from the stormy showers,
And laugh the troublous winds and angry sky,—
Piping, Lah'! might I live, and piping might I die!

And would my lucky fortune so grace me,
As in low Cranbrook, or high Brenchly's hill,
Or in some cabin near thy dwelling, place me,
There would I gladly sport and sing my fill,
And teach my tender Muse to raise her quill;
And that high Mantuan shepherd's self to dare,
If aught with that high Mantuan shepherd mought compare.

Phineas Fletcher

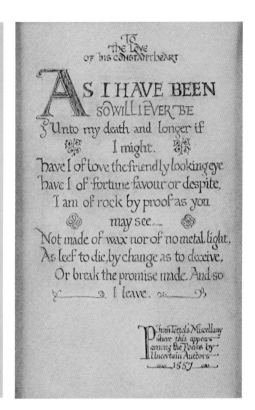

To
the Love
Of his constant heart

AS I HAVE BEEN
so will I ever be
Unto my death and longer if
I might.
Have I of love the friendly looking eye
Have I of fortune favour or despite.
I am of rock by proof as you
may see.
Not made of wax nor of no metal light,
As leef to die, by change as to deceive,
Or break the promise made. And so
I leave.

From Tottel's Miscellany
where this appears
among the Poets by
Uncertain Auctors
1557

ABOVE: From Vita's writing desk: Chris
St John's transcription of *Laetemur in Ea*,
presented to Vita on the anniversary of their
meeting, August 1933.

ABOVE: From Vita's Writing Room: Chris
St John's transcription of 'To the love of his
constant heart', December 1933.

ABOVE: This tiny photograph of Chris
St John, Vita's lover in 1932, was formerly
displayed on the writing desk.

Gwen St Aubyn

1933–1940

Equally significant is the portrait by Lenare of the woman who supplanted Christopher St John in Vita's heart: Gwen St Aubyn, Harold's sister and Vita's loving companion at Sissinghurst from 1933 to 1940. Severely injured in a car accident in July 1933, Gwen required brain surgery, and her doctor recommended rural seclusion for her recovery period. Leaving her husband and five young children in London, Gwen sought refuge with her brother and his wife at Sissinghurst. Ten years younger than Harold, Gwen seemed on the surface to have little in common with Vita; intensely religious, she was considering conversion to Catholicism, and writing a book on family life. Somewhat to their surprise, the sisters-in-law fell in love; Vita told Chris St John the relationship had started as a joke, deepening quickly to intense physical attraction. Vita made a bedroom for Gwen in the Tower, immediately above the Writing Room. For seven years, their lives were intimately entwined.

Family photograph albums record Gwen being carried up to the Tower on a stretcher after one of her many operations, and there are countless shots of the pair sitting in the garden, or on the steps to the Tower, with their respective children, dogs and puppies. Both Harold and Gwen's husband, Sam, appear in some of these images, apparently at ease with what must have been an increasingly difficult situation. In the early days illness provided the explanation for Gwen's prolonged presence at Sissinghurst. Vita wrote to Virginia in August 1933 apologising for her failure to visit Rodmell: 'The point is that I've got my sister-in-law staying here, and I am supposed to provide the cure. Country rustication and all that. And Harold is writing a book about Lord Curzon, whereas I am not writing any book at all, so I am free to look after his sister, which I like doing.'

After another brain operation in January 1934, Gwen's doctor advised that she was still far from well, and explained to her husband that she needed rest away from her five children, Giles, Philippa, Piers, John and Jessica, then aged from eight to fifteen. Harold claimed that Sam seemed 'quite sensible about it. He quite sees that Gwen must be left to make her own arrangements, and not [be] bothered by obligations, domestic or otherwise.' While Harold went to Paris with James Lees-Milne, Vita took Gwen to Italy, staying in the same Italian castle where Elizabeth Von Arnim had set her novel *The Enchanted April*. Chris St John, aching with jealousy, described this trip as their 'honeymoon', and Gwen wrote to Harold that she was 'happier than I have ever been in all my life. You see for once I have no responsibilities, Vita having taken them all'.

It was on this holiday that Vita began to write her erotic novel *Dark Island*, described by Leonard Woolf as 'perilous fantastic stuff, a woman flagellated in a cave, how much will the public stand?' Dedicated to Gwen, the book is very obviously set on St Michael's Mount, the castellated Cornish island to which Sam St Aubyn was heir. The hero, Venn, harbours a sadistic passion for the heroine Shirin – Vita's pet name for Gwen. Shirin's friend Christina stumbles across a cave hidden at the base of the island, and discovers 'the

RIGHT: Gwen St Aubyn by Lenare, from Vita's writing desk.

ABOVE: Souvenir of Gwen and Vita's visit to Timgad in North Africa.

TOP: Abstract design of flowers by Duncan Grant, embroidered by Gwen St Aubyn while living at Sissinghurst.

RIGHT: The oak table beside Vita's daybed, inset with Gwen's embroidered panel.

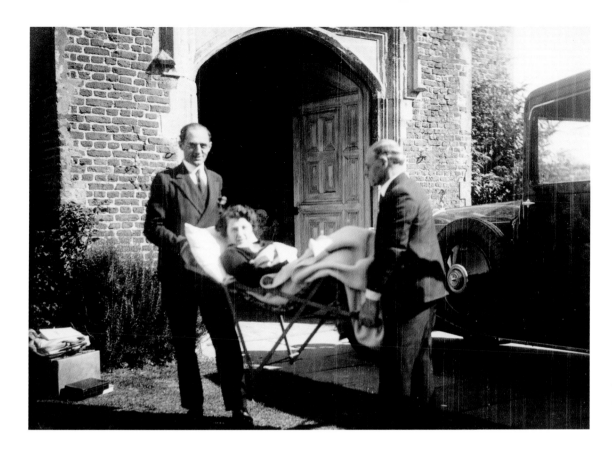

naked body of Shirin chained against the rock. Arms outstretched as of one crucified, Shirin stood there on a ledge, lashed and bound to the iron rings provided for Venn's boats. And Venn himself, crouching, ready to spring, watched her, with a switch in his hands.'

Harold was worried about the book's sadistic content: 'I hope you do not get disagreeable reviews my darling. I feel rather doubtful about that book somehow ... All I mean is sadism is a subject about which I do not care to read.' He was also frustrated by the feminist ideas Vita was encouraging in his sister: 'Gwen, for instance, thirty years ago would have felt fortunate at having a faithful husband and five adoring children. But now she feels that these obligations limit herself, that there is a more important function for her somewhere beyond the function of wife and mother.' Instead of returning home, Gwen concentrated on her own work (*The Family Book*, published in 1935),

and smartening up Vita, who started wearing lipstick and brightly coloured silk shirts. Virginia was deeply disapproving: 'She has grown opulent & bold & red – tomatoe [sic] coloured, and paints her fingers and lips which need no paint – the influence of Gwen.' Gwen's name pops up in countless letters between husband and wife, quietly involved in activities at Sissinghurst – 'measured the central path in the Kitchen Garden and Gwen helps me' – and taking on the role of mediator. Sometimes her efforts were fruitless: to Harold's chagrin, Gwen failed to persuade Vita to attend a dinner at Buckingham Palace in honour of the King of Romania – 'She said I would be wrong to funk it – and that I *must* go. But I am too shy and also I do think it wrong to spend all that money for one evening.'

During these years Gwen and Vita travelled together to Scotland, France, Italy and North Africa, sleeping in tents in the Sahara

ABOVE (ALL): Gwen and Vita at Sissinghurst with dogs
and puppies, 1930s.

Desert, and visiting dramatic sites like Timgad and Touggourt in Algeria – 'Darling,
I think Touggourt is one of the most magical places I ever struck ... The sun is so hot
that, like everyone else, we have been obliged to wear solar topees, and Gwen is wearing
cotton frocks.' Gwen converted to Catholicism while she was living at Sissinghurst, and
Vita became interested in religious subjects. Together they researched the contents
for saintly biographies: firstly St Joan of Arc, then St Teresa of Avila and St Thérèse of
Lisieux (published together as *The Eagle and the Dove*). Gwen wrote a book recording her
conversion – *Towards a Pattern: Letters to a Friend*, which is dedicated to Vita. Traces
of Gwen pervade Vita's Writing Room; like Virginia Woolf, she loved embroidery; Vita
obtained Duncan Grant patterns for her to work on, and the oak table by Vita's daybed is set
with a vibrant example. These were happy times for both of them, absorbed in Sissinghurst,
dogs, and family life. Virginia Woolf described seeing Vita at Sissinghurst in 1935: 'she has
grown very fat, very much the indolent county lady, run to seed, incurious now about books;
has written no poetry, only kindles about dogs, flowers, and new buildings ... and there is no
bitterness ... only a certain emptiness.'

ABOVE: Vita and the boys with Gwen St Aubyn and
her husband Sam, sitting outside South Cottage.

ABOVE: The ruins of Timgad, one of Vita and Gwen's favourite sites in Algeria.

LEFT: Vita's photograph of Gwen in a tent in the Sahara Desert.

TOP LEFT: Ben, Harold and Gwen sitting outside the Tower, 1933.

The South Cottage

1930–1933

If the Tower was Vita and Gwen's domain, the South Cottage belonged to Harold. Harold's Sitting Room and Study dominate the ground floor; the atmosphere is immediately warm and welcoming, evocative of his personality and interests. Books line the oak-panelled walls, soft rugs cover the floor, and comfortable sofas jostle with favourite pieces from Long Barn. A pair of 15th-century Italian male and female saints with shimmering golden backdrops stand either side of a verdant tapestry, exactly as they had done in the 'Big Room' which he had loved at Long Barn. Each of these images depicts a happy partnership: the tapestry shows a shepherd teaching a shepherdess how to play the pipes, and the saints were thought by the Nicolsons to be Mary and Joseph. Over the fireplace hangs a Flemish picture of a smiling Pomona, goddess of fruitful abundance, surrounded by the fruits of a plentiful harvest; naked cupids cavort in the background, playing with goats and grapes.

Harold's Sitting Room feels like the perfect place for a fireside conversation, glass in hand, latest gossip at the ready. This was a man who loved weekends with the Rothschilds at Waddesdon, revelling in the roses, hot water and huge lunches. He liked to stay with Somerset Maugham at Cap Ferrat, and motor with Lord Berners through Italy. He loved good food and fine wines, and by the 1930s was beginning to burst out of his expensive clothes. A contemporary noted how Harold's 'splendid frogged top-coat with Persian lamb collar, well-tailored, double-breasted blue serge suit and blue shirt' would often be let down by 'fly buttons wide open, displaying two prominent shirt tails'. His friend Ann Lindbergh enjoyed hearing his voice on the radio: 'He still speaks in that pleasant, half-humorous and rather effeminate accent of cynical sideline detachment, but you can feel his emotions.' Vita was often comforted on sleepless nights by listening to his broadcasts; the writer and broadcaster St John Ervine admired 'the sleepy insolence of his style, the slight thickness of his utterance, the reluctant way in which he begins his talk with "Er, good evening"'.

Looking beyond the comfortable furnishings, more subtle themes begin to emerge. On the mantelshelf below Pomona stands a drawing of Byron, and two original manuscripts: Byron's last words written at Missolonghi, and a note written to his school friend Lord Clare, referring to 'a childish misunderstanding, the only one which ever arose between us ... I retain this note solely for the purpose of submitting it to his perusal, that we may smile over the recollection of our first and last quarrel.' According to his biographer James Lees-Milne, Harold had been in love with Lord Byron for years, fulfilling a heartfelt dream in 1924 with the publication of his study of Byron's last days in Greece. He later participated in men-only 'Byron nights', colluding with fellow Byron author Peter Quennell in the suppression of those parts of Byron's correspondence which revealed his bisexuality. 'When one is "queer" one is reluctant to claim great men as being "queer" also,' he commented.
Also on the mantelshelf was a manuscript of Oscar Wilde's poem,

RIGHT: Harold's Sitting Room in South Cottage.

San Miniato, and amongst the 2,000 books on the surrounding shelves first editions of *De Profundis* and *The Importance of Being Earnest*. In addition to Byron, Harold had written studies of three other sexually ambiguous writers – Verlaine, Tennyson and Swinburne – and their works all feature at Sissinghurst. Harold's library is very obviously the collection of a former diplomat and author, reflecting his interests in political as well as literary history. As his son Nigel remarked in *A Long Life*, 'it was sometimes held against him that he never made up his mind what sort of man he was, a writer who dabbled in politics, or a politician with a literary bent.' Nearly all the books bear dates and inscriptions in Harold's hand, and many contain momentoes: into his 14-volume set of Byroniana, for example, is slotted a Greek picture postcard of Byron, a ticket to the Keats-Shelley memorial in Rome, and a ticket to the 1924 Byron centenary dinner.

A simple oak shelf is set into the wall below the window in the Study, and on it sits his Remington portable typewriter. When in between jobs, Harold spent intense periods at Sissinghurst writing: six months in 1932, producing his novel *Public Faces*; two months in 1934, writing the biography of American politician Dwight Morrow. He had his portrait painted by Eddy's friend, Ian Campbell-Gray, and bought contemporary pictures from two of Eddy's lovers: a view of Venice by Duncan Grant, and a homo-erotic scene by John Banting, featuring two naked men lying either side of a screen (see page 135). In these cosy and conducive surroundings Harold 'achieved a different and no less self-indulgent form of elegance which seemed to me likely to survive in my own lifetime. It consisted of comparatively modest establishments in the country and in London, and a gay combination of the Café Royal, Bloomsbury, rooms in the Temple, the Travellers Club, the garden at Sissinghurst, foreign travel, the purchase of books and pictures and the unthinking enjoyment of books and wine.'

ABOVE: Harold's Sitting Room in South Cottage – the view through the doorway to the fireplace.

ABOVE: Harold's overmantel: a painting of Pomona, surrounded
by the fruits of harvest and dancing cupids.

ABOVE: Harold's drawing of Byron, and a Byron manuscript, propped on the mantelpiece.

ABOVE: A painting of the 'Big Room' at Long Barn.

ABOVE: Portrait of Harold by Ian Campbell-Gray.

LEFT: Harold in Cap Ferrat with Somerset Maugham.

ABOVE: Looking into Harold's Study, South Cottage.

LEFT: Harold's writing shelf in the Study.

Harold and Vita's Bedrooms

Harold and Vita's 'modest establishment' was extended in 1933 to create a new bedroom for Harold on the first floor of South Cottage, just across the landing from Vita. This replicated their arrangements at Long Barn, where husband and wife had slept in adjoining rooms, calling out 'hello neighbour' to each other in the morning. The fittings were carefully considered: Harold slept in a beautiful polychrome French 17th-century style bedstead, transferred from the best spare room at Long Barn. His bedroom walls were lined with panels of hand-painted 18th-century Chinese wallpaper, inherited from his Irish grandmother. One of the rare pieces of Nicolson heritage at Sissinghurst, these conveyed happy memories of childhood holidays at Shanganagh Castle. Sadly only one section survives today, preserved carefully in a frame. In its place hang other images connected to Harold, including a watercolour of 'Marmaduke Bonthrop Shelmerdine', his character in *Orlando*.

Vita's Bedroom was formed within the surviving corner fragment of the 1570s house, and she was delighted when the workmen discovered 'the most lovely, huge, stone Tudor fireplace'. She asked for all the plaster to be carefully removed, revealing the soft original brickwork. Tapestries of hunting scenes were hung against the bare brick, along with paintings of flowers and fruit. There were touches of Lady Sackville: glass sunbursts were fixed to the wall, and giant green ceramic fruits and vegetables arranged on the polychrome side cabinet. Many features link back to the Renaissance bedroom Vita had created with Rosamund Grosvenor at Knole, and only dismantled after her father's death in 1928. The carved walnut Italian bed is made up from 17th-century Cassone pieces, and is thought to have come from Knole, possibly specially put together for Vita. On the windowsill sits the medieval boy bishop's head from the niche beside her fireplace at Knole. Near it stands a crucifix, and two illuminated religious manuscripts made for Vita by a reverent Chris St John: the Pater Noster, and the Oblatio Sui – 'Take O Lord, All my Liberty'.

It was in this room, on 10 August 1932, that Chris St John fell deeply and irrevocably in love with Vita: 'Contemplating a worn piece of green velvet on her dressing table, I felt my whole being dissolve in love. I have never ceased to love her from that moment.' Chris recognised the shrine-like quality of the space, decked by Vita with embroidered religious silks which crumbled to the touch. She responded to Vita's sadness – 'a tragic figure ... All this beauty of environment, and she is not happy'. Embroiled, at a time, in a complex triangular relationship with Evelyn Irons and her partner Olive Rinder, Vita had just learned of Evelyn's defection to a new lover. She later found Olive a cottage near Sissinghurst, and helped her financially. Harold wrote sympathetically, 'I do hope O.R. is better – poor wounded little chaffinch, so plucky'. On 11 August, the day after Chris's visit, Vita posted a poem to Evelyn entitled *Valediction*:

RIGHT: Harold's Bedroom, South Cottage.

ABOVE: Vita's Bedroom, photographed on the day she died.

RIGHT: Vita's Bedroom in South Cottage.

ABOVE: Harold's bedside table, South Cottage.

ABOVE: The framed Chinese Wallpaper from Shanganagh Castle.

Do not forget, my Dear, that once we loved.
Remember only, free of stain or smutch,
That passion once went naked and ungloved,
And that your flesh was startled by my touch.

Mourning the loss of Evelyn, Vita dallied briefly with the adoring Chris. Their physical relationship was brief, but the emotional impact lasted many years. As Chris ruefully recorded, there had come into Vita's life 'a person, much older than herself, who had fallen in love with her at first sight. This love might well have seemed to her foolish, almost ridiculous, if there had not been something in the way it was expressed which appealed to her sense of beauty. My letters charmed her, she was interested in the person who wrote them. It is probable too that sated with a series of superficial Lesbian love affairs with very feminine women, the relationship with a woman of a different type, capable of entering into her intellectual and spiritual life, fulfilled a need. "What is it you wish?" "What can I do for you?" I think that was in her mind. Her gratitude impelled her to feign the love I sought.'

RIGHT:
Vita's Bedroom, the
polychrome side cabinet.

LEFT: The windowsill in Vita's Bedroom, with Chris St John's illuminated text of the Pater Noster, a bust of Harold, and a crucifix.

Christopher St John

Vita had no compunction in toying with the affections of those already involved in longstanding partnerships. Chris lived at nearby Smallhythe Place in what Vita described as a 'triptych' with Ellen Terry's daughter, Edith 'Edy' Craig, and the artist Clare 'Tony' Atwood. All three were strong independent professional women, who had been actively involved in the campaign for women's suffrage. Edy had founded the Pioneer Players, a subscription theatre company which mounted plays with feminist themes. Tony was one of the few female artists to be officially commissioned during the First World War, and examples of her work could be seen in the Imperial War Museum and the Tate. Chris was an Oxford-educated journalist who had worked for the first women-only weekly newspaper – *Time and Tide* – and later established a career as a biographer. At the time she met Vita, Chris had been commissioned to produce the life of Dr Christine Murrell, the first female member of the General Medical Council.

Chris, Tony and Edy were part of a wide lesbian circle, many of whom chose to adopt masculine dress or masculine names, and live openly with their partners. Dr Murrell, for example, also used the name 'Christopher', and lived in a ménage-à-trois with Dr Honor Bone and Marie Lawson. Radclyffe Hall – 'John' – and her partner Una Troubridge were close friends, spending Christmas with the Smallhythe trio, and nearly deciding to build a house in the field behind their garden. Vita and Virginia, by contrast, led more closeted lives, their sexual identities cloaked by marriage and the apparent maintenance of heterosexual households. Chris St John summed up some of these contradictions in a letter to Vita: 'I can never think of your sex, only of your humanity. I could love you in breeches, or in skirts, or in any other garments, or in none. I know you must be a woman – evidence your husband and your sons. But I don't think of you as a woman, or as a man either. Perhaps as someone who is both, the complete human being who transcends both.'

Chris never spoke of her distress when Vita transferred her affections to Gwen in July 1933, but Edy and Tony both realised what was going on. Edy was surprisingly sympathetic – 'What I don't understand is why you

ABOVE: Gwen with Edy, Chris and Tony, 1939.

RIGHT: Edy, Chris and Tony on their first visit to Sissinghurst, 10 August 1932.

weren't prepared for it. I'm told it's her way to take people up and drop them ... Don't take it so hard, and don't blame her, she doesn't see any harm in it. It's a sort of "droit de seigneur" with her.' Edy carried on inviting Harold and Vita to performances in the Barn Theatre she had set up at Smallhythe, involving them in her fundraising activities. As time progressed the trio gradually resumed their visits to Sissinghurst, and Vita returned to Smallhythe to dine with them. After Edy's death, Vita left a moving description of their independent personalities, and the distinctive home they created together:

This is the remarkable thing about them: all three of them are still persons on their own. Strong personalities, living at such close quarters for so many years, yet none of them has been extinguished by the other ... Now let us go indoors ... Edy sits there at the head of her refectory table. She sits in a big oak chair, with a dim mirror behind her, reflecting her white hair and the shoulder of her red smock ... There are red cushions, and some red velvet, and candlelight, and shining horse-brasses, and pottery bowls with oranges on the table. Edy presides. Christopher and Tony sit in any seat they can find down the long table. They are all three very much at their ease in this their dining-room: its colour and its lighting match their mellow mood. They talk. It is enchanting talk; it ranges widely; it isn't always consecutive; it starts too many hares too quickly to follow up; they argue, they quarrel; they interrupt. It is impossible to have any sequence of conversation. Yet how stimulating it is! And how friendly! how [sic] lively! ... what a sense of life one gets from them.

RIGHT: Chris St John's illuminated manuscript of the Oblatio Sui, July 1935.

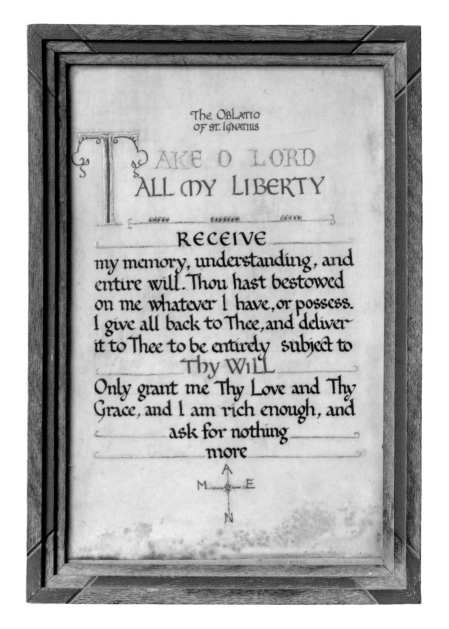

ABOVE: Tony Atwood's portrait of Vita as Portia.

LEFT: Tony Atwood's portrait of the family at Smallhythe; Edy Craig in the blue cap, Chris St John seated at the rear.

Emotional Choreography

While Vita spent most of the year at Sissinghurst, Harold's presence was intermittent, usually appearing only at weekends. In the early days, Vita's lover Evelyn Irons resented making way for Harold: 'not that I disliked him. But I had to go back to London on Saturday mornings, because he was coming by the next train for the weekend. As both he and Vita agreed that she would have her girl-friends while he had his boys, I didn't see the need for all this concealment, but Vita was determined to keep our relationship under wraps.' There may have been another reason for this unusual discretion. Harold was at a low ebb during the early 1930s, having left the *Evening Standard* to work briefly and unsuccessfully for Oswald Mosley's 'New Party'. Here he overlapped with Eddy's friend John Strachey, and the ebullient bisexual MP Bob Boothby, who appears in photographs at Sissinghurst.

Optimistically declaring: 'I am still very promising and shall continue to be so until the day of my death', Harold was in fact beginning to feel middle aged, overweight and lacking in direction. Although a popular broadcaster, his books never achieved Vita's sales figures, and he missed the buzz of diplomatic life. Further blows to his confidence came in 1933. In May, the Woolfs came for lunch at Sissinghurst, and Ben suddenly blurted out in front of them that Lady Sackville had told him both his parents were homosexual, and that his mother had slept with Virginia and Violet, and his father with boys in Tehran. Virginia erupted, 'the old woman ought to be shot'. In July, Harold's sister Gwen moved full-time to Sissinghurst, diverting Vita's attention, and disrupting the normal rhythm of their life.

Gwen encouraged him to seek another public role, and in 1935 Vita's cousin Earl De La Warr came to the rescue, nominating Harold for the safe National Labour seat of West Leicester. Harold joined a group of MPs who trod the same tightrope – carefully concealing their private lives in order to avoid exposure and prosecution. His friends included Chips Channon, Victor Cazalet, Jack Macnamara and Ronnie Cartland. Another MP, Robert Bernays, became Harold's great love of the late 1930s. They spent an idyllic ten weeks in Africa on a parliamentary delegation in 1937. Harold told Vita about 'my beloved Rob', and Bernays wrote to his sister, 'he is very fond of me as I am of him', and that he hoped one day to marry a woman with whom he had 'the kind of mental affinity I have with H'.

During these years Harold was introduced to the Soviet spy Guy Burgess, who nearly became his private secretary. According to Ben's diary: 'He will look up a few things for Daddy and get political experience in exchange – no money transactions.' Burgess actually decided to work for Harold's friend Jack Macnamara, on slightly more exacting terms: Goronwy Rees claimed the duties of Jack's assistants 'combined those of giving him political advice and satisfying his emotional needs'. Harold kept in touch with Burgess for years, becoming a fascinated observer of his difficult relationship with

ABOVE RIGHT: Harold and Nigel at Sissinghurst, 1930.

RIGHT: Harold, Virginia Woolf and Ben by the lake at Sissinghurst, 1933.

James Pope-Hennessy: 'I do not think that the affair is going very well, and James looks white and drawn. I am seeing him alone on Wednesday and he will tell me all about it. Guy is a bit of a scamp, and James is far too sensitive and affectionate for that sort of relationship.'

Burgess's Russian handler produced a report in 1939 which summarises the contradictions of the secretive world he and Harold shared: 'Many features of his character can be explained by the fact that he is a homosexual. He became one at Eton, where he grew up in an atmosphere of cynicism, opulence, hypocrisy and superficiality ... Part of his private life is led in a circle of homosexual friends whom he recruited among a wide variety of people, ranging from the famous liberal economist Keynes and extending to the very trash of society down to male prostitutes.' Burgess's dancer boyfriend Jack Hewitt met Harold many times at their flat, and found himself cross-questioned in a very unparliamentary way. Jack dismissed Harold as 'a pink and white candyfloss of a man who, when he did speak to me, always brought the subject round to masturbation. He wanted breathlessly to know how many times a week I did it. A patronising bore.'

RIGHT: Harold's friend the bisexual MP Bob Boothby (right) at Sissinghurst with Ben (left) and the author Malin Sorsbie (centre).

ABOVE: Harold's friend Guy Burgess, lover of
James Pope-Hennessy.

LEFT: Harold's great love of the late 1930s,
Rob Bernays, MP.

The Long Library
1935

In spring 1935 Harold and Vita finally completed the one large space at Sissinghurst they had always planned for entertaining. Their architect Albert R. Powys was Secretary of the Society of the Protection of Ancient Buildings, and gently restrained any ambitions they might have had for more dramatic alterations. He was not amused when Harold suggested decorating the new North Courtyard wall with niches, ready to contain the busts by German artist Paul Hamann which had been made from life masks of Harold's friends in Berlin. If it had been followed through, this wall of British Worthies (rivalling the similar feature at Stowe) would have been set with the head of Harold alongside Raymond Mortimer, Eddy Sackville-West, Paul Hyslop, Dorothy Wellesley, David Herbert and Edward Knoblock.

Mindful of budget, the Nicolsons contented themselves with carving a drawing room cum library from the former stables and saddle room in the South Wing. Designed together, it was executed apart, in a pattern which mirrored their increasingly segregated personal lives. While Gwen and Vita were driven slowly back from Rome by the chauffeur, Copper, visiting places associated with Joan of Arc, Harold supervised the builders on site. Walls were knocked down, a large window inserted, and a fireplace created from fragments of an Elizabethan one found in the gardens. Harold worried about the proportions – 'it will always have about it a feeling of a hospital ward in some Turkish barracks.'

Harold then embarked on his own holiday in Paris and Venice with former lover Victor Cunard, leaving Vita and Gwen to cheer the room up with appropriate contents. Places were found for all the most impressive Nicolson wedding presents, moved from house to house since 1913: the huge writing desk given by Lord Sackville was placed on the dais; a painted red-and-white 18th-century cupboard to the left of the fireplace, and a beautiful lacquer Coromandel cabinet to the right. This had once stood in the Entrance Hall at Ebury Street, and was the backdrop for the first photograph taken of Ben with his proud father. The pair of replica 17th-century ebony mirrors, with their elaborate silver mounts, went at either end of the room.

Lady Sackville had supplied them with a copy of Kneller's portrait of Charles Sackville, 6th Earl of Dorset, and a host of other treats: electrotype copies of silver sconces and a silver chandelier from Knole; a rent table topped

RIGHT: The Long Library, Sissinghurst.

ABOVE: The Long Library – Lady Sackville's lapis lazuli-topped table in the foreground, with the walnut Vestal Virgin by Toma Rosandić to the rear.

TOP RIGHT: The Coromandel Cabinet.

RIGHT: Harold with baby Ben, photographed in front of the Coromandel Cabinet at Ebury Street.

with lapis lazuli; a huge oak table with a green faux marble top which she had used as her dining table in Brighton; a bowl of life-sized carved exotic fruit, and a bizarre chair in the style of Andrea Brustolon with human figures holding up the arms. The entrance wall was lined with nearly 4,000 books, mostly first editions sent to Vita and Harold to review. Only one modernist piece intrudes on the otherwise stately surroundings: the walnut original of Toma Rosandić's sinuous Vestal Virgin. Harold placed a lead version of this statue at the centre of the White Garden in 1935, carrying it precariously across the courtyards with the help of Ben and Francis Graham-Harrison.

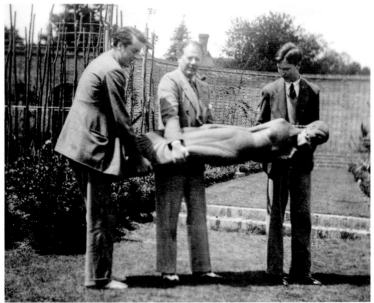

ABOVE: A painted cupboard, given to Harold and Vita as a wedding present by Sir Louis Mallet.

TOP LEFT: View of the Long Library from the 1930s.

FAR LEFT: Lead version of the Vestal Virgin by Toma Rosandić in the White Garden.

LEFT: Harold, Ben and Francis Graham-Harrison carrying the Vestal Virgin.

'Loss of friendly light': The Onset of War
1938–1942

Try as they might, the Nicolsons were never entirely happy with the new space – 'This is a note of warning: the big room is a failure ... I just can't seem to get it to come together'. They fiddled about, adding panelling to the fireplace wall in 1937, but never grew to love it. Less than a year later, war with Germany seemed imminent, and Vita wrote to Ben describing the strange precautions they had been advised to take for the safety of the Sissinghurst community: 'Making the big room into a gas-proof shelter meant that sheets of asbestos were screwed all over the windows ... and that the fireplace was similarly blocked and that piles of blankets were stacked ready to nail over all the doors. It meant I had to shift all the red amber and the Persian pots, and otherwise make the room ready for the sudden occupation by old Mrs Hayter, Mrs Copper, Fay, Mrs Farley, Mrs Adsett, young Adsett and so on.'

Along with the threat of war came emotional change. Vita had a brief affair with her secretary, Mac, and in 1940 Gwen moved out of the Tower at Sissinghurst, and into Horserace Cottage, a short walk away across the fields. Vita's sense of loss was palpable, and found expression in sections of her long poem *The Garden*, written between 1939 and 1945:

LEFT: Vita in the Writing Room at Sissinghurst, 1939, photographed by Gisele Freund

War brings this seal of peace,
This queer exclusion,
This novel solitude,
This rare illusion.

As to the private heart
All separate pain
Brings loss of friendly light
But deeper, darker gain.

Left truly alone for the first time since Gwen's arrival in 1933, Vita became depressed, drinking more than usual and worrying Harold by appearing blotchy and muddled in the middle of the day. Her depression deepened in 1941 when she learned of Virginia Woolf's suicide, less than a month after they had spent time together at Rodmell. Harold understood her despair – 'My dearest, I know that Virginia meant something to you which nobody else can ever mean and that you will feel deprived of a particular sort of haven which was a background comfort and strength. I have felt sad about it every hour of the day.'

On 8 April 1941, Vita paid her last visit to Monk's House. She found Leonard alone: 'He was having his tea – just one tea-cup on the table where they always had tea. The house full of his flowers and all Virginia's things lying about as usual. He said let us go somewhere more comfortable, and took me up to her sitting-room. There was her needlework on a chair and all her coloured wools hanging over a sort of little towel-horse that she had made for them. Her thimble on the table. Her scribbling-block with her writing on it. The window from which one can see the river. I said Leonard, I do not like you being alone like this. He turned those piercing blue eyes on me and said it's the only way.'

Deprived of both Virginia and Gwen, who finally left Sissinghurst to join her husband at St Michael's Mount in 1942, Vita relied increasingly on Harold for support. Her letters reveal heartfelt appreciation for their unconventionally inclusive union:

I was thinking to myself, as one does think when one is alone and doing something mechanical like putting dahlias into a trug, I was thinking 'How queer! I suppose Hadji and I have been about as unfaithful to one another as one well could be from the conventional point of view, even worse than unfaithful if you add in homosexuality, and yet I swear no two people could love one another more than we do after all these years'.

RIGHT: Gwen sitting in military uniform on the steps of the Tower, 1939.

FAR RIGHT: The Tower at Sissinghurst, where Vita remained alone following Gwen's departure to Horserace Cottage in 1940.

Bibliography

Adair, Joshua, 'One must be ruthless in the cause of Beauty': Beverly Nichols' and John Fowler's Queer Domesticity in Mid-Century England (*Visual Culture and Gender*, Vol 5, 2010)

Adlard, Eleanor (ed.), *Edy, Recollections of Edith Craig* (Frederick Muller, 1949)

Anscombe, Isabelle, *Omega and After, Bloomsbury and the Decorative Arts* (Thames & Hundson, 1981)

Baker, Michael, *Our Three Selves: A Life of Radclyffe Hall* (William Morrow & Co, 1985)

Barlow, Clare, *Queer British Art 1867–1967* (Tate Publishing, 2017)

Bell, Quentin and Nicholson, Virginia, *Charleston: A Bloomsbury House & Garden* (Frances Lincoln, 1997)

Bloch, Michael, *Closet Queens: Some Twentieth Century British Politicians* (Little, Brown, 2015)

Brown, Jane, *Vita's Other World – A Gardening Biography of Vita Sackville-West* (Viking, 1985)

Caws, Mary Ann and Nicolson, Nigel (ed.), *Vita Sackville-West, Selected Writings* (Palgrave, 2002)

Cockin, Katherine, *Edith Craig (1869–1947): Dramatic Lives* (Cassell, 1998)

Cockin, Katherine, *Edith Craig and the Theatres of Art* (Bloomsbury, 2017)

Cohen, Lisa, *All We Know: Three Lives* (Farrer, Strauss & Giroux, 2012)

Connolly, Cressida, *The Rare and the Beautiful, The Lives of the Garmans* (4th Estate, 2004)

Crab, John, *Decadence: A Literary Anthology* (British Library, 2017)

Dally, Peter, *Virginia Woolf: The Marriage of Heaven and Hell* (Robson Books, 1999)

Davis, Whitney, 'Homoerotic Art Collection from 1750 to 1920' (*Art History*, Vol 24, No.2, April 2001)

De la Noy, Michael, *Eddy: The Life of Edward Sackville-West* (Bodley Head, 1988)

Dejardin, Ian and Milroy, Sarah (ed.), *Vanessa Bell* (Philip Wilson, 2017)

Dennison, Matthew, *Behind the Mask: The Life of Vita Sackville-West* (William Collins, 2015)

Desalvo, Louise and Mitchell, Leaska (ed.), *The Letters of Vita Sackville-West and Virginia Woolf* (Cleiss Press, 2004)

Dunn, Jane, *Virginia Woolf and Vanessa Bell – A Very Close Conspiracy* (Virago, 2001)

Gillespie, Diane Filby, *The Sisters' Arts, The Writing and Painting of Virginia Woolf and Vanessa Bell* (Syracuse University Press, 1988)

Glendinning, Victoria, *Leonard Woolf: A Life* (Simon & Schuster, 2006)

Glendinning, Victoria, *Vita – The Life of Vita Sackville-West* (Penguin Books, 1984)

Hamer, Emily, *Britannia's Glory, A History of Twentieth Century Lesbians* (Cassell, 1996)

Hancock, Nuala, *Charleston & Monk's House: The Intimate House Museums of Virginia Woolf and Vanessa Bell* (Edinburgh University Press, 2012)

Helt, Brenda and Detloff, Madelyn (ed.), *Queer Bloomsbury* (Edinburgh University Press, 2016)

Humm, Maggie, *Snapshots of Bloomsbury: The Private Lives of Virginia Woolf and Vanessa Bell* (Rutgers University Press, 2005)

Humm, Maggie (ed.), *Virginia Woolf and the Arts* (Edinburgh University Press, 2010)

Hogarth, Mary, *Modern Embroidery* (The Studio, Spring Number, 1933)

Holroyd, Michael, *Lytton Strachey: The New Biography* (Pimlico, 2011)

Knights, Sarah, *Bloomsbury's Outsider: a Life of David Garnett* (Bloomsbury, 2015)

Lee, Hermione, *Virginia Woolf* (Vintage, 1997)

Lees-Milne, James, *Harold Nicolson: A Biography, Vols 1–2.* (Chatto & Windus, 1981)

Lehmann, John, *Leonard and Virginia Woolf at Monk's House,* (National Trust Studies, 1985)

Lehmann, John, *Virginia Woolf and her World* (Harvest, 1977)

Light, Alison, *Mrs Woolf and the Servants* (Penguin, 2008)

Lownie, Andrew, *Stalin's Englishman: The Lives of Guy Burgess* (Hodder, 2016)

MacCarthy, Fiona and Collins, Judith, *The Omega Workshops 1913–1919 – Decorative Arts of Bloomsbury* (Crafts Council, 1984)

Melville, Joy, *Ellen and Edy* (Pandora Press, 1987)

Newman, Michael, *John Strachey (Lives of the Left)* (Manchester University Press, 1989)

Nicolson, Adam, *Sissinghurst: An Unfinished History* (HarperPress 2009)

Nicolson, Nigel, *Portrait of a Marriage: Vita Sackville-West and Harold Nicolson* (Weidenfeld & Nicolson, 2001)

Nicolson, Nigel (ed.), *Vita and Harold: The Letters of Vita Sackville-West and Harold Nicolson 1910–1962* (Weidenfeld & Nicolson, 1992)

Nicholson, Virginia, *Among the Bohemians: Experiments in Living 1900–1939* (Penguin, 2003)

Noble, Joan Russell (ed.), *Recollections of Virginia Woolf by her Contemporaries* (Penguin, 1972)

Partridge, Frances, *Julia: A Portrait of Julia Strachey by Herself and Frances Partridge* (Gollancz, 1983)

Potvin, John, *Colour Wars: Personality, Textiles and the Art of the Interior in 1930s Britain* (Visual Culture in Britain, 2015)

Rachlin, Ann, *Edy was a Lady* (Matador 2011)

Raven, Sarah, *Vita Sackville-West's Sissinghurst: The Creation of a Garden* (Virago, 2014)

Reed, Christopher, *Bloomsbury Rooms: Modernism, Subculture and Domesticity* (Yale University Press, 2004)

Reed, Christopher, 'Design for (Queer) Living: Sexual Identity, Performance and Décor in British Vogue, 1922–26' (*GLQ: A Journal of Lesbian and Gay Studies*, 12:3, 2006)

Rose, Norman, *Harold Nicolson* (Jonathan Cape, 2005)

Rothenstein, John, *Summer's Lease: Autobiography 1901–1938* (Holt, Rinehart & Winston, 1966)

Sackville-West, Edward, *Ruin: A Gothic Novel* (W. Heinemann, 1926)

Sackville-West, Vita, *Dark Island* (Hogarth Press, 1934)

Sayers, Janet, *Art, Psychoanalysis and Adrian Stokes: A Biography* (Karnac Books, 2015)

Sheean, Vincent, *Personal History* (Doubleday, Doran and Company, 1935)

Shone, Richard, *Bloomsbury Portraits* (Phaidon, 1976)

Slocombe, Emma, *The Reluctant Heir – Edward Sackville-West at Knole* (National Trust Collections Annual, 2016)

Souhami, Diana, *The Trial of Radclyffe Hall* (Doubleday, 1999)

Spalding, Frances, *Duncan Grant: A Biography* (Pimlico, 1998)

Spalding, Frances, *The Bloomsbury Group* (National Portrait Gallery, 2014)

Spalding, Frances, *Virginia Woolf: Art, Life and Vision* (National Portrait Gallery, 2014)

Spalding, Frances, *Paper Darts: The Letters of Virginia Woolf* (Collins & Brown, 1991)

Sturgis, Matthew, *Passionate Attitudes: the English Decadence of the 1890s* (Macmillan, 1995)

Taylor, D.J, *Bright Young People: The Lost Generation of London's Jazz Age* (Farrar, Straus and Giroux, 2010)

Thomas, Hugh, *John Strachey* (Harper & Rowe, 1973)

Thompson, Noel, *John Strachey: An Intellectual*

Biography (Macmillan, 1993)

Todd, Pamela, *Bloomsbury at Home* (Abrams, 2000)

Williams-Ellis, Amabel, *All Stracheys are Cousins* (Littlehampton, 1983)

Woolf, Leonard, *Downhill All the Way: An Autobiography of the Years 1919–1939* (Mariner Books, 1989)

Woolf, Virginia, *A Room of One's Own* (Hogarth Press, 1929)

Woolf, Virginia, *Orlando* (Hogarth Press, 1928)

Woolf, Virginia, *The Diary of Virginia Woolf*, edited by Anne Oliver Bell and Andrew McNeillie, Volumes 1–5 (Hogarth Press, 1977–84)

Woolf, Virginia, *The Letters of Virginia Woolf*, edited by Nigel Nicolson and Joanne Trautmann, Volumes 2–6, (Hogarth Press, 1976–80)

Yoss, Michael, *Raymond Mortimer: A Bloomsbury Voice* (Bloomsbury Heritage, 1998)

Picture Credits

Sources of Quotations

All quotations from the writings of the following: Edward Sackville-West by kind permission of Richard Shone; Duncan Grant © Estate of Duncan Grant, all rights reserved DACS 2018; *The Diary of Virginia Woolf*, Volume I by Virginia Woolf, edited by Anne Olivier Bell, published by The Hogarth Press. Reproduced by permission of The Random House Group Ltd. ©1977; ibid, Volume II ©1978; ibid, Volume III ©1980; ibid, Volume IV ©1982; ibid, Volume V ©1984; 'The question of things happening', *The Letters of Virginia Woolf*, Volume II 1912–22, edited by Nigel Nicolson, published by The Hogarth Press. Reproduced by permission of The Random House Group Ltd. ©1976; 'A change of perspective', *The Letters of Virginia Woolf*, Volume III 1923–28, edited by Nigel Nicolson, published by The Hogarth Press. Reproduced by permission of The Random House Group Ltd. ©1977; 'A reflection of the other person', *The Letters of Virginia Woolf*, Volume IV 1929–31, edited by Nigel Nicolson, published by The Hogarth Press. Reproduced by permission of The Random House Group Ltd. ©1978; 'The Sickle side of the Moon', *The Letters of Virginia Woolf*, Volume V 1932–35, edited by Nigel Nicolson, published by The Hogarth Press. Reproduced by permission of The Random House Group Ltd. ©1979; 'Leave the letters till we're dead', *The Letters of Virginia Woolf*, Volume VI 1936–41, edited by Nigel Nicolson, published by The Hogarth Press. Reproduced by permission of The Random House Group Ltd. ©1980; Leonard Woolf with permission from the University of Sussex and the Society of Authors; Vita Sackville-West reproduced with permission from the Literary Estate of Vita Sackville-West; Harold Nicolson reproduced with permission from the Literary Estate of Harold Nicolson; Nigel Nicolson reproduced with permission from the Literary Estate of Nigel Nicolson; John Rothenstein reproduced with permission from the Rothenstein estate; James Lees-Milne by kind permission of Michael Bloch; Julia Strachey © Julia Strachey Estate; John Lehmann © Estate of John Lehmann; Elizabeth Bowen © Estate of Elizabeth Bowen; Adrian Stokes © Estate of Adrian Stokes. While every effort has been made to contact copyright holders of all material reproduced in this book, if we have inadvertently omitted any, please contact the publishers who will be pleased to provide acknowledgements in future editions.

Introduction

p7 Michael De-la-Noy, *Eddy, The Life of Edward Sackville-West*,1988 p111; Indiana University Library, Sackville-West V MSS, correspondence, Box 2, July 1919– June 1926; ibid; Virginia Woolf, Letter 1524 to Jacques Raverat, 24 January 1925; Jane Garrity & Tirza True 'Queer Cross-Gender Collaborations' in *Cambridge Companion to Gay and Lesbian Writings*, ed Hugh Stevens, 2011, p185; Virginia Woolf, *A Room of One's Own*, 1929, p6; Vita Sackville-West, 27 September 1920, quoted in: Nigel Nicolson, *Portrait of a Marriage*, 1973 p101.

Eddy Sackville-West, Knole, 1926

p10 Michael De-la-Noy, *Eddy*, *op.cit.* p5-6; ibid; Virginia Woolf, *Orlando*, 1928, Penguin Edition 1993, p12; Indiana University Library, Sackville-West V MSS, correspondence, Box 2, July 1919–June 1926; **p15** John Rothenstein, *Summers Lease*, 1965 p76-7; ibid, p63-4; ibid p78; ibid, p87; ibid, p73; Hugh Thomas, *John Strachey*, 1973 p7; **p18** Michael De-la-Noy *op.cit.* p72; ibid; Hugh Thomas *op.cit.* p24; **p19** John Rothenstein, *op.cit.* p91; **p20** Virginia Woolf, Letter 1524 to Jacques Raverat, 24 January 1925; **p22** Janet Sayers, *Art, Psychoanalysis and Adrian Stokes, A Biography*, 2015, p23; Virginia Woolf, Letter 1534 to Jacques Raverat, 5 February 1925; ibid; **p25** ibid; book review of 'Paul Morand', *Vogue*, early March 1924 p63; **p26** Frances Partridge, *Love in Bloomsbury*, 1988 p138; Frances Partridge, *Julia, A Portrait of Julia Strachey, by herself and Frances Partridge*, 1983 p129–30; De-la Noy *op.cit.* p107; **p30** Victoria Glendinning, *Vita, the life of Vita Sackville-West*, 1983 p151; John Rothenstein *op.cit* p76; **p32** ibid, p151; ibid, p217; De-la-Noy *op.cit.* p42; ibid p44; ibid, p111; ibid, p124–5; **p33** letter from Duncan Grant to David Garnett, 6 April 1926, quoted in Frances Spalding, Duncan Grant, footnote 26, Chapter 16; letter from Duncan Grant to Eddy Sackville-West, July 1926, British Library RP 9336; letter from Duncan Grant to Eddy Sackville-West, 2 August, 1926, British Library RP 9336; **p36** De-la-Noy *op.cit.* p15; ibid, p111; **p38** 'Unity in Diversity, the Home of Mr Osbert and Mr Sacheverell Sitwell', *Vogue* late October,1924; ibid; De-la-Noy *op.cit.* p81; ibid, p81; Virginia Woolf, Letter 1624 to Vita Sackville-West, 16 March 1926; **p40** D.J. Taylor, *Bright Young People*, 2008 p172; De-la-Noy *op.cit* p136–7; letter from Eddy Sackville-West to Duncan Grant, 31 March 1927; Frances Partridge, *Love in Bloomsbury*, *op.cit.* p153. **p42** Frances Partridge, *Julia*, *op.cit.* p138; **p46** De-la-Noy *op.cit.* p54; Emma Slocombe,

'The Reluctant Heir, Edward Sackville-West at Knole', *National Trust Historic House & Collections Annual* 2016, p22; VS. Ezema, A.C. Arenji, A.G. Ohubuenyi, 'Implications of Friedrich Nietzsche's Master-Slave Morality in Interpersonal Relationship', *European Journal of Social Science*, Vol 55, No3, September 2017 p262–274; Eddy Sackville-West, *The Ruin*, 1927, facing title page; ibid; p121; **p49** ibid, p49; **p52** De-la-Noy *op.cit.* p6; Virginia Woolf, Letter 1524 to Jacques Raverat, 24 January, 1925; Virginia Woolf, Diary, 18 November, 1924; De-la-Noy *op.cit.* p115. **p54** Virginia Woolf, Diary, 4 April 1930. Frances Partridge, *Love in Bloomsbury*, *op.cit.* p172; ibid; ibid; ibid; **p56** De-la-Noy, *op.cit.* p.166; ibid p169; Ibid p171; Virginia Woolf, Letter 3543 to Vita Sackville-West, 19 August 1939; Ben Nicolson, Diary, September 1939.

Virginia Woolf, Monk's House, 1928

p60 Garrity & True, *op.cit.*; Jane Dunn, Virginia Woolf and Vanessa Bell, *A Very Close Conspiracy*, 2000 p229; Virginia Woolf, Diary, 10 August 1927; Virginia Woolf, Diary, 9 June 1926; Virginia Woolf, Letter 2020 to Vanessa Bell, 24 April, 1929; John Lehmann, 'Leonard and Virginia Woolf at Monk's House', in *Writers at Home*, National Trust Studies, 1985 p162; ibid, p159; **p65** Victoria Glendinning, *Vita*, *op.cit.* p181; Virginia Woolf, Letter 1647 to Vanessa Bell, 13 June 1926; Virginia Woolf, Letter 1820 to Vita Sackville-West, 8 October, 1927; Virginia Woolf, *Orlando*, 1928 p76; ibid p218; ibid p73, ibid **p68** Virginia Woolf, Diary, 14 March 1927; Virginia Woolf, Letter 1893 to Vanessa Bell, 9 May 1928; James Douglas, *Daily Express* editorial 'The Book that must be suppressed', 19 August 1928; ibid; Virginia Woolf, Letter 2218 to Ethel Smyth, 15 August 1930; **p69** ibid; Havelock Ellis, *Studies in the Psychology of Sex, Sexual Inversion*, 1915; Virginia Woolf, *Orlando, op.cit* p132–3; **p70** Virginia Woolf, Diary, 3 July 1919; Virginia Woolf, Letter 1073 to Katherine Arnold-Forster, 12 August 1919; Virginia Woolf, Letter 1075 to Margaret Llewellyn Davies, 17 August 1919; Angelica Garnett, *Deceived with Kindness*, 1995 p251; John Lehmann *op.cit.* p159; Victoria Glendinning, Leonard Woolf, *A Life*, 2006 p309. **p71** Victoria Glendinning, *Vita, op.cit.* p137; **p73** Pamela Todd, *Bloomsbury at Home*, 2001, p31; Vanessa Bell, *Sketches in Pen and Ink, a Bloomsbury Book*, ed Lia Giachero, 1997 p105; Leonard Woolf, *An Autobiography*, 1911–69, Oxford University Press edition 1980 p21. **p76** Virginia Woolf, Letter 1450 to Jacques Raverat, 8 March 1924; Virginia Woolf, Letter 1456 to Janet Case, 12 April 1924; William Plomer,

The Autobiography, 1975 p249; *Vogue*, Early November 1924, 'Modern English Decoration, Some Examples of the Interesting Work of Duncan Grant and Vanessa Bell'; ibid; Virginia Woolf, Letter 2016 to Vanessa Bell, 7 April 1929; Virginia Woolf, Diary, 9 January 1924; Vanessa Bell, letter to Quentin Bell, 22 June 1930; Lisa Cohen, Three Lives, 2012, p247; ibid p247; **p78** Joan Russell Noble, *op.cit.* p171; Lisa Cohen, *op.cit.* p258; *Vogue*, late January 1925, p40, Polly Flinders on 'Marie Laurencin'; ibid; **p79** Lisa Cohen, *op.cit.* p258; Joan Russell Noble, *op.cit.* p178; Lisa Cohen, *op.cit.* 265; ibid p266; ibid; **p82** Virginia Woolf, Letter 1760 to Vanessa Bell, 22 May 1927; Virginia Woolf, Diary, 9 June 1926; Virginia Woolf, Diary, 4 July 1927; Virginia Woolf, Letter 2599 to Ethel Smyth, 18 and 19 June 1932; Virginia Woolf, Diary, 18 December 1928; **p84** Virginia Woolf, Letter 2011 to Vanessa Bell, March 1929; ibid; Virginia Woolf, Letter 2669 to Lady Ottoline Morrell, 25 November 1932; Christopher Reed, *Bloomsbury Rooms*, 2004 p272; ibid; Virginia Woolf, Diary, 4 December 1932; Christopher Reed *op.cit.* p272; ibid; ibid; **p90** Quoted in Virginia Woolf, Diary, 12 September 1921; Joan Russell Noble, *op.cit.* p168; ibid, p178; Virginia Woolf, Diary, 28 June 1923; John Lehmann, *op.cit.* p 162; Joan Russell Noble, *op.cit.* p58; Virginia Woolf, Letter 3056 to Ethel Smyth, 10 August 1935; **p92** Virginia Woolf, Diary, 8 August, 1928; **p93** Victoria Glendinning, *Vita*, *op.cit.* p163; **p94** Victoria Glendinning, *Leonard Woolf op.cit.* p274; Joan Russell Noble, *op.cit.* p49; Virginia Woolf, Letter 2194 to Ethel Smyth, 22 June 1930; Joan Russell Noble, *op.cit.* p168. **p96** Virginia Woolf, Diary, 11 June 1922; National Trust Guidebook Monk's House, 1998, p 5; Virginia Woolf, *A Room of One's Own, op.cit.* p6; Virginia Woolf, Diary, 28 March 1929; Virginia Woolf and the Arts, ed. Maggie Humm 2010, Chapter 10 'Virginia Woolf and Monk's House' by Victoria Rosner p183; Virginia Woolf, Diary, 8 December 1929. **p98** Virginia Woolf, Diary, 24 August 1933; Virginia Woolf, Letter 2244 to Ethel Smyth, 28 September 1930; Virginia Woolf, Letter 1773 to Vanessa Bell, 8 June 1927; Virginia Woolf, Letter 3649 to Hugh Walpole, 29 September 1940; Virginia Woolf, Diary, 20 October 1940. **p99** Virginia Woolf, Diary, 20 October 1940.

Vita Sackville-West, Sissinghurst, 1930
p106 Vita Sackville-West, *Journal of the Royal Horticultural Society*, November 1953; Vita Sackville-West, *Sissinghurst*, published 1931; Vita Sackville-West, 'Sissinghurst Castle', *Country Life*, 3 September 1942; Khalil Gilbran, *The Prophet*, 1923; Norman Rose, *Harold*

Nicolson, 2006 p139; **p108** Nigel Nicolson, *Long Life*, 1997, p210; **p112** Vita & Harold, *The Letters of Vita Sackville-West & Harold Nicolson 1910-62*, ed Nigel Nicolson, p195, Vita Sackville-West, *The Edwardians*, 1930, Virago Press edition 2013 p59–60; Norman Rose *op.cit.* p48; Harold Nicolson, *The Desire to Please*, 1943 p4; Norman Rose *op.cit.* p6; Vita Sackville-West, *Selected Writings*, 2002 p59; **p116** Victoria Glendinning, *Vita op.cit.* p95; **p118** Virginia Woolf, Diary, 4 July 1927; Victoria Glendinning, *Vita, op.cit.* p88; Virginia Woolf, Diary, 21 December 1924; Catalogue of the Collection at 40 Sussex Square, Brighton June 1923, Messrs Wilson & Co.; **p120** Jane Brown, Vita's Other World, 1985 p116; ibid; ibid, p57; **p121** Press cutting in Vita & Harold's Marriage photograph album at Sissinghurst (illustrated p123); ibid; Victoria Glendinning, *Vita, op.cit.* p247; **p127** ibid p170; Norman Rose *op.cit.* p95; ibid; ibid p137; ibid p159; Virginia Woolf, Letter 1780 to Vita Sackville-West, 4 July 1927; Victoria Glendinning, *Vita op.cit.* p178. **p128** Cressida Connolly, *The Rare and the Beautiful, The Lives of the Garmans*, 2005 p82; Victoria Glendinning, *Vita op.cit.* p185; ibid p180; ibid p206; ibid; ibid p36; ibid; **p129** ibid p41; ibid; Inventory of Contents of The South Cottage, Sissinghurst, taken by Nigel Nicolson, 1985; Victoria Glendinning, *Vita, op.cit.* p54. **p132** ibid, p220–1; James Lees-Milne, Harold Nicolson, A Biography Vol 1 1981 p382; ibid; Michael Bloch, *Closet Queens*, 2015 p164. **p136** James Lees-Milne, *Harold Nicolson, op.cit.* p389; Victoria Glendinning, *Vita, op.cit.* p188; James Lees-Milne, *People and Places: Country House Donors and the National Trust*, 1992 p168; Victoria Glendinning, *Vita, op.cit.* p217. **p138** James Lees-Milne, Harold Nicolson, *A Biography*, Vol II p9; Jane Brown, *op.cit.* p109; ibid; **p139** Adam Nicolson, *Sissinghurst, An Unfinished History*, 2009 p235; ibid p236; Jane Brown, *op.cit.* p110. **p141** Vita Sackville-West, *Sissinghurst, op.cit.*; Victoria Glendinning, *Vita, op.cit.* p233; ibid p235; ibid p236; Adam Nicolson, *op.cit.* p284; Victoria Glendinning, Vita, *op.cit.* p202; **p142** ibid p239; ibid p242; ibid; **p143** Cressida Connolly *op.cit.* p78; Glendinning, *Vita, op.cit.* p201; ibid; **p144** Virginia Woolf, Letter 2862 to Vita Sackville-West, 5 March 1934; ibid; **p152** Vita Sackville-West, Letter to Virginia Woolf, 18 August 1993, Berg Collection, New York Public Library; Victoria Glendinning, *Vita, op.cit.* p267; Christopher St John, *History for V.S.W.*; Glendinning, *op.cit.* p269; Virginia Woolf, Diary, 17 July 1934; Vita Sackville-West, *Dark Island*, 1934 p246; **p155** Victoria Glendinning, *Vita, op.cit.* p273; ibid p270; Virginia Woolf, Diary, 17 July 1934; Harold Nicolson, Diary, 27 September 1933; *Vita*

& Harold, op.cit.; p308; **p156** ibid p291; Virginia Woolf, Diary, 11 March 1935; **p158** Norman Rose *op.cit.* p185; James Lees-Milne, *Harold Nicolson, op.cit.* Vol II p105; ibid p4; quoted in: Countess Guccioli, *My Recollections of Lord Byron*, 1869 p148; Peter Cochran, *Byron's Romantic Politics*, 2011 p147; **p160** Nigel Nicolson, *Long Life, op.cit.* Chapter 1; Norman Rose *op.cit.* p248; **p164** ibid; Victoria Glendinning, *Vita, op.cit.* p235; A catholic prayer of dedication to Christ, ascribed to St Ignatius of Loyola, 1491–1556; Christopher St John, *History for V.S.W,* quoted in Victoria Glendinning, *Vita, op.cit.* p250; ibid; ibid p249; **p166** Vita Sackville-West, *Valediction*, 1932; **p170** Christopher St John, letter to Vita Sackville-West 10 November 1932, quoted in: Victoria Glendinning, *Vita, op.cit.* p253; Christopher St John, *History for V.S.W. op.cit.*; **p172** Edy, *Recollections of Edith Craig*, ed Eleanor Adlard, 1949 p123–4; **p174** letter from Evelyn Irons to Victoria Glendinning, 9 Sept 1981, quoted in: Victoria Glendinning, *Vita, op.cit.* p240-1; Norman Rose, *op.cit.* p184. Nigel Nicolson, *Portrait, op.cit.* p170; Michael Bloch, op.cit p173; ibid; ibid; Ben Nicolson, Diary, 25 March 1936, quoted in Andrew Lownie, *Stalin's Englishman, The Lives of Guy Burgess*, 2016 p62; **p174** Goronwy Rhys, *Chapter of Accidents*, 1972 p122; **p176** *Vita & Harold, op.cit.* p340; Andrew Lownie, *op.cit.* p56; Jack Hewit unpublished memoir, quoted in Andrew Lownie, *op.cit.* p347; **p178** Victoria Glendinning, *Vita, op.cit.* p278; **p183** ibid; Vita Sackville-West, letter to Ben Nicolson, 9 October 1938; Vita Sackville-West, *The Garden*, 1939–45; *Vita & Harold, op.cit.* p337; Victoria Glendinning, *Vita, op.cit.* p315. **p184** *Vita & Harold, op.cit.* p339.

PICTURE CAPTIONS
p10 Virginia Woolf, *Orlando*, 1928, Penguin Edition 1993 p12; **p20 (right)** original photograph caption from Lady Ottoline Morrell's photograph album, handwritten, National Portrait Gallery. **p22** Janet Sayers, *op.cit.* p110; 'Unity in Diversity, The Home of Mr Osbert and Mr Sacheverell Sitwell', *Vogue* late October 1924; **p39** ibid.; **p.67** (left) Original caption to this illustration when used in Virginia Woolf, *Orlando*, 1928; (photo p66) Victoria Glendinning, Vita, *op.cit.* p171.; **p.131** (photo p130, left) Vita Sackville-West, letter to Harold Nicolson, 15 February 1913; *Vita & Harold, The Letters of Vita Sackville-West and Harold Nicolson*, ed Nigel Nicolson, *op.cit.*, 1992 p35. **p.136** Jane Brown, *Vita's Other World*, 1985 p110.

Index

Numbers in italic refer to illustrations

Acknowledgements

My thanks go first of all to Robert Sackville-West, Adam Nicolson, Juliet Nicolson and Vanessa Nicolson for giving permission to study the private collections and archives at Knole and Sissinghurst, and for their generous help in reading chapters of this book while it was in progress. I am also profoundly indebted to the National Trust staff who provided access to archive and research material held at Knole, Monk's House, Sissinghurst and Smallhythe and in the regional research archive at Scotney Castle: Emma Slocombe, Helen Fawbert, Alison Pritchard, Clare Reed, Helen Davis, Vicky McBrien and Susannah Mayor.

In the early stages of the book I was grateful for the help of Professor Richard Sandell and Dr Matt Smith of Leicester University, who worked with Tom Freshwater and Rachael Lennon to develop the Trust's 2017 Prejudice and Pride programme, celebrating the 50-year anniversary of the partial de-criminalisation of homosexuality in the UK. Richard Sandell, Oliver Garnett and David Taylor kindly provided comments on the text as it developed, and Christopher Rowell and Tim Pye supplied additional information on the collections.

This publication was made possible by the National Trust's Specialist Publications Programme, supported by a generous bequest from the late Mr and Mrs Kenneth Levy. Special thanks must also go to Hannah Kay, Hester Liarkos and Pauline Wall, General Managers of Knole, Monk's House, Sissinghurst and Smallhythe, for their support of this book and the Prejudice and Pride programme. I am sincerely grateful to the Trust's Publisher, Katie Bond, and to Claire Forbes, Specialist Publications Editor, for all their input and advice. At Pavilion Books, I am indebted to Susan Swalwell, who commissioned the book, managing editor Sophie Nickelson and designer Lee-May Lim. Susannah Stone provided inventive picture research, and John Hammond took beautiful new photography at Knole and Sissinghurst.

Finally, a great many thanks go to Jessica McCarthy and Amanda Vinnicombe for their encouraging support, to Alexandra Harris for providing stimulating feedback, and to Harry and Cas for bearing with me as I followed in the footsteps of previous Stracheys, and buried myself in Bloomsbury.